THE OPEN
1960-1990

A photographic record featuring the work of Bert Neale

Text by Michael Hobbs
Picture Editor: D Rogers
Editor: R Bickersteth

The Pipkin Press

Many of the photographs which illustrate this book are the work of
the pioneering Golf Photographer, Bert Neale.

His understanding of golf, and his familiarity with both players and courses enabled
him to produce photographs which captured the emotion and beauty of the game.

Bert was easily recognised by his red beret 'trade mark' and has been
sadly missed by us all since his death at Christmas 1989.

However his photographs live on, and the Bert Neale Collection forms
a lasting tribute to a fine photographer.

Bob Thomas
May 1991

CONTENTS

A BRIEF HISTORICAL BACKGROUND

Tom Morris, Bob Andrew, Willie Park, Alex Smith, Willie Steel, Charlie Hunter, George Brown, Andrew Strath. Going out in pairs, with a marker, this was the handful of professionals which set forth on 17 October 1860 in what is recognised as the first Open Championship.

They were to play three rounds stroke play over the twelve-hole Prestwick links. The local favourite was Tom Morris, professional to the Prestwick club, and the event was thought to lie between him, Willie Park, Andrew Strath and Bob Andrew.

As it turned out, there were only two men in it – Morris and Park. After a first round of 55, Park had a three-stroke advantage on Morris, who made little headway as the three rounds were played out between noon and dusk. Park was declared the winner, with Morris two strokes adrift. The prize was the championship belt of red morocco leather with silver buckle, and, of course, the title 'champion golfer'. There was no prize money.

St Andrews in the 1850's

Prestwick Golf Club was quite a newcomer on the golfing scene, founded as recently as 1851, but it was go-ahead. It had, for example, brought Tom Morris over from St Andrews to be its professional. In 1856 Prestwick also wrote to other clubs suggesting a championship for golf professionals. There seems to have been little enthusiasm for the idea and in 1860 the club decided to go it alone, timing the event to coincide with Prestwick's autumn meeting, one of the two biggest occasions in the life of the club.

But that 1860 event wasn't 'open' to all. No amateurs played and the entry would have been entirely restricted to Scottish professionals except that Blackheath, near London, requested that George Daniel Brown be allowed to play.

In 1861 the event became fully open. Eight amateurs entered and there was a slightly increased entry from over the border. Once again, the contest was primarily a battle for supremacy between Morris and Park. The latter held the lead most of the way until failure to carry some dunes cost

Old Tom Morris

Willie Park

him three strokes. Morris won by four and did a great deal better the following year, taking the championship by 13 strokes from Park.

Those early years of were consistently a Morris versus Park contest, with Park returning to form in 1863, and so preventing Morris from winning the belt outright with three successive victories.

Although Morris won again in 1864, Andrew Strath was becoming a name to be reckoned with. He was fourth in 1863 and finished second the next year, a couple of strokes behind Morris. In 1865 he took the title by two strokes from Park. How great a figure he might have become must remain speculation because, like so many in those times, he died tragically young .

After 1867 Morris had four wins and Park three, but their dominance was coming to an end. Tommie Morris, son of the man later to be referred to as Old Tom, was making his way up the lists. In 1866, at the age of fifteen, he was 9th and the next year 4th behind his father. In 1868 he began with a round of 51, followed with a 54 and finished the day with a remarkable 49. His total was 154, good enough for a five-stroke victory. It also beat the previous championship best by eight strokes. The seventeen-year-old was already clearly the greatest player golf had yet seen.

In 1869 he won again, after a tie with his father, and his finest performance came in 1870. He eclipsed previous records with an opening round of 47 and followed with a couple of 51s. His 149 total was, once more, comfortably a record and his twelve-stroke margin over the second-placed men is clear evidence of his supremacy. In future years, while the twelve-hole course remained in use, no one came nearer than eight strokes of his championship-winning aggregate and his 47 for a round was even more invincible. Tommie's third victory in a row marked the end of an era – he had won the championship belt outright. Perhaps no one had realised that a trophy which had cost the enormous sum of £25 would have so short a life!

Young Morris was producing golf at least a class better than had been seen before. In addition, he was an evolutionary player. Instead of the very long, flat St Andrews swing which swept the ball on its way, Morris swung, so they say, shorter and more furiously. He may also have been the first player to find a new use for the rut

iron (a small-headed club intended for removing the ball from ruts and cartwheel tracks). Morris used it for pitching too, a risky shot because of that very small head which made the shank so likely. On the greens, putting off the back foot so that the ball was airborne for the first part of its travel, he was a bold and deadly holer-out with excellent touch from longer range.

There was no championship in 1871, but early the following year Prestwick once more took the lead. This time they suggested the championship be renewed on three courses – Musselburgh, St Andrews and Prestwick itself. Agreement was reached. The claret jug, still the trophy today, was commissioned at a cost of £30. As it was to be a perpetual trophy, each champion would have a gold medal to keep, plus the sum of £8.

Harry Vardon

The first name to be inscribed on the jug was Tommie Morris, giving him four successive victories by the age of 21, a feat still unequalled.

With no more worlds left to conquer there seems to have been a decline in the young man's powers, for he failed to win at St Andrews and Musselburgh in the next few years. In 1875 he did not enter, his wife having recently died in childbirth. On Christmas morning that same year he was found dead. There can only be speculation as to whether his top form would ever have returned.

In retrospect, the championship is often thought to have entered an anti-climactic phase after the death of the brief comet. Even so, Jamie Anderson came close to duplicating Morris's feat with three wins between 1877 and 1879. In 1880 he didn't play because, so the story goes, there was very short notice of the date of the championship.

Bob Ferguson won that year and again in 1881 and 1882. He came even closer to a fourth successive victory – tying with Willie Fernie after the four rounds of nine holes at Musselburgh. After a further 36 holes in the play-off, Fernie was champion – by just one stroke.

The Open was now becoming a bigger event. Fifty-two played

at St Andrews in 1888, 48 at Musselburgh the next year and then at Prestwick in 1890 – the drop due solely to the fact that western Scotland was considered a long journey from the main golfing centres along the east coast of the country.

Nevertheless, this last year was significant. For the first of only six occasions throughout the history of the event, an amateur, John Ball from Hoylake, won. Even more horrifying for the Scottish professionals of the day, he was also the first Englishman to take the title.

The omens for the Scottish professional looked even bleaker when another Hoylake amateur, Harold Hilton, won at Muirfield in 1892, the first time the championship was extended to 72 holes.

In the event, however, the emergence of the English threat was far more long-lasting than that of amateurs. Though Hilton was to win

Harry Vardon

again, the only other amateur to take the championship was the most dominant golfer of them all – Bobby Jones.

If the 'foreign' threat may have seemed momentary it was soon a fact. Willie Auchterlonie won in 1893. No Scottish-born, bred and resident golfer has won in the almost hundred year period since . . .

This was a watershed year in another sense also. It saw the first championship entries of both J H Taylor from Westward Ho! and Harry Vardon from Jersey. Taylor created a great impression in the days leading up to the championship at Prestwick and began with a

James Braid

brilliant found of 75, the lowest of the whole championship by three strokes (only four others broke 80 in any of the four rounds).

Thereafter he faded and Harry Vardon at no point made any impact.

It was a different story at St George's, Sandwich in 1894 – the first time the championship was played outside Scotland. Taylor was in close contention throughout and in the end cruised home by five strokes. The era of what was to be called 'The Great Triumvirate' had begun.

Taylor won again the following year and in 1896 tied with Vardon, losing the play-off. Two of the Triumvirate had arrived. The third, James Braid, came close in 1897, but Harold Hilton won over his home course, Hoylake – the fifth course to join the championship rota.

The century ended with two more Vardon victories and Taylor also raised his total to three championships in 1900. These two were having a great impact on people's notion of how the game ought to be played. Taylor amazed with his steadiness in the long game and the accuracy of his approach shots. Vardon changed ideas about the plane of the golf swing and was the first upright swinger. With no apparent effort – a great contrast to most, if not all, his contemporaries – he hit a long ball and reckoned to lay his fairway woods close to the hole.

It seemed that these two would dominate the game of golf for years to come, but they were quickly joined by the third member of the Triumvirate: James Braid, a Scot. Although he hit the ball with what one journalist called "divine fury", no one element of his game aroused quite the admiration attracted by Taylor or Vardon. All three, however, helped to alter drastically ideas about how the golf club should be held.

Previously, the club was usually held in a palm – not finger – grip, often with both thumbs being off the shaft. At the top of the back-swing most loosened hold, to allow more freeom, and re-gripped coming back to the ball – hardly a sure recipe for consistency. Early this century, the Triumvirate's playing methods were closely studied and the so-called Vardon Grip, which was used by all three, became the fashion – and remains so today. (The essential item was thought simply to be the overlapping of the little finger of the right hand on the first finger of the left. It took a great deal longer for the impor-tance of retaining a firm grip throughout the swing to be accepted.)

Braid won his first title in 1901, with Vardon and Taylor second and third. Few interrupted the dominance of these three in the years leading up to the First World War. One who did was Alex Herd in 1902, the first champion to abandon the gutty and use a rubber-cored ball. Another was Arnaud Massy, a Frenchman and the first overseas player to win the Open (1907).

When the war ended championships until 1920, Braid and Taylor had won five times, with Vardon one ahead on six victories. He remains the only player to achieve this tally. Despite the hiccup of Massy's win, British dominance of the Open Championship remained complete. A few Americans, such as Johnny McDermott and Francis Ouimet, had tried their luck but made no real impression.

After the long years of war, the days of the Triumvirate were over. Each was about fifty years-old. George Duncan and Abe Mitchell seemed set to replace them, especially after Mitchell won an unofficial Open in 1919 and Duncan became champion in 1920 with the top US player, Walter Hagen, 54th.

The very next year, however, the first American-based golfer, Jock Hutchison, won in his former home town of St Andrews. Walter Hagen then proceeded to underline US supremacy by finishes of first, second, first between 1922 and 1924. British supporters could only console themselves with the thought that Hagen wasn't quite the complete golfer. He hit his share of wild long shots, though no one could match his skills from 100 yards off the flag and in putting.

Then came Bobby Jones, whom even Hagen could never manage to beat in stroke play. Jones first entered while over to play in the first amateur international between Britain and America in 1921. Playing badly at St Andrews, he tore up his card. He was nineteen. His return was delayed several years, though he quickly established himself as the greatest American player with wins in both the US Amateur and Open Championships.

As an amateur he could spare limited time for golf because of degree studies, followed by establishing himself as a lawyer. His next visit to Britain came in 1926. He failed to do himself justice in the Amateur Championship and that decided him to stay on for the Open.

Bobby Jones

He won. Jones thought it right to defend his title so found the time to return in 1927. Again he was champion. The next two titles went to Hagen but Jones wasn't in the field either year. In 1930, however, Jones decided that the Grand Slam of the Amateur and Open titles of Britain and the United States was just a possibility, however remote.

He did it. In succession he won the British Amateur at St Andrews, the Open at Hoylake, the US Open at Interlachen and the US Amateur at Merion.

That same year he retired from all competitive golf – having, incidentally, won the British Open every time he'd entered in his mature years. No one could deny that this was the most complete golfer the game had seen. There was the drowsy rhythm of his long game and his touch on and around the greens was superb. He was also the most effective competitor of all and seemed, someone commented, "to be trying twice as hard as anyone else." Through his career in tournament golf, which began at the age of fourteen, until his retirement at 28, he won about half of only some 50 events he entered.

With Jones gone and Hagen into the twilight of his career, British prospects didn't seem to improve as Americans Tommy Armour, Gene Sarazen and Densmore Shute took the next three titles (1931-33). At least Armour was Scottish-born.

But a new British star was on the rise – Henry Cotton. However, he seemed able to get himself into contention, only to fade. He did so again in 1934, finishing with a 79. But before that he had put the Sandwich field to the sword with rounds of 67, 65 and 72. He was miles ahead and even that 79 was still good enough for a five-stroke victory.

Henry Cotton

With that win, American dominance of the championship was gone . . . for the time being. Until the Second World War all the champions were British, with Cotton taking his second title in 1937 when the whole of the US Ryder Cup team was in the field.

The first post-war championship was played at St Andrews in 1946 and won by American Sam Snead. His comment afterwards that the Open was "just another tournament" was a common US attitude. For US Tour players, the Open, and golf in general outside the United States, had no real appeal. Their Tour was where the money was.

For the rest of the world, however, the Open Championship continued to be the leading event, and especially so for British and Commonwealth golfers.

Max Faulkner

In 1948 Cotton won his third Open. It's some indication of his status at this time that he was the only British player since the Triumvirate to win the title more than once. In the forty years since, only Nick Faldo has won it twice, although his two Masters titles, and perhaps more achievements in majors yet to come, will give him a higher placing even than Cotton.

South African Bobby Locke, fresh from many titles on the US Tour, won in 1950 and 1952. In between, Englishman Max Faulkner won – and proved to be the last British Isles player to do so for many a year.

Locke was an unlikely-looking champion, mainly because he seemed so unathletic. Heavy-jowled and the image of a portly, middle-aged gentleman, his victories world-wide are mainly the result of a steady long game (despite breaking not a few of the technical 'rules') and mastery of the wedge and putter.

Hard upon Locke's heels was the young Australian Peter Thomson – whose time was coming. In 1952 he was second behind Locke and joint second the following year, this time behind Ben Hogan, whose career record in championship was to be perfect, if limited: played one, won one.

Bobby Locke

Peter Thomson

In 1954 Thomson took his first title at Birkdale and then followed with consecutive victories at St Andrews and Hoylake. He was the first to win three in a row since Bob Ferguson in 1882. Could he equal young Tommie Morris and make it four?

Almost. In 1957 he was second behind Locke, enjoying his last hurrah. In 1958, however, Thomson made it four out of five, an achievemnt only bettered by Morris, back in 1872. Like Jones on his retirement, Thomson was still only 28. Surely he would go on to eclipse Harry Vardon's record of six Open titles? He made the game look as easy as he himself declared it was, and went about his business with a smile and not the least sign of the pressure he may have been feeling.

But times were about to change. In 1958, only one American name figures amongst the final scores – that of Gene Sarazen, in his late 50s. He had made the trip to play in the World Seniors Championship and also to see old friends. In the wings, though, was a crop of young men poised to take golf into a new era, and in particular there was the modern equivalent of the Great Triumvirate – the Big Three: Palmer, Player, Nicklaus.

1959

THE OPEN

Fred Bullock – one of the early leaders

This was one of so many opens when unknowns have made the early pace. The rule of thumb for deciding what is really going to happen at the climax is to note which of the stars have not virtually destroyed their chances in the first round. If they've gone round in par, or thereabouts, they know that everything is still to play for. The inexperienced usually fade away in the unaccustomed spotlight of press and public attention.

Arnold Stickley and Fred Bullock, with 68s, were the unknown first round leaders in this instance and after the second day Bullock was still there on 138. Perhaps an even greater surprise was that Peter Thomson, having headed the 36-hole pre-qualifying stage, only just made the 36-hole cut in the championship proper, on 148. He had not been so far out of contention even on his first appearance back in 1951.

Going into the final round Bullock was still in the lead, together with Sam King, and the young South African Gary Player, having made a significant move in his third round, was four behind them.

Player was out in 34 and with birdies at the 10th, 16th and 17th needed a par 4 at the 427 yard 18th to set a stiff target. Alas, he bunkered his tee shot and followed by taking three putts for a 6. Legend has it that Player was in tears immediately afterwards. Certainly, there are pictures to back up this claim (see following page), showing a very depressed young man.

However, as the afternoon wore on, player after player faded away. Finally, the Belgian Flory van Donk - the best continental player of the times - needed a birdie 3 to tie with Gary's total. He took 5 and the South African was champion for the first time.

It was a considerable surprise. When Player first appeared in Britain in 1955 he was an earnest young man, given to asking advice about his swing and professional prospects. He was usually told that he should find some other line of work and just play golf for fun. His swing was flat, his grip faulty. He seemed to have little rhythm or feel for the game. Such comments were probably true. Even today, Player is apt to finish off balance on full shots and his jabbing technique in the short game wouldn't suit many. However, his early advisers hadn't reckoned on his willingness to work and work and work on the practice ground, his persistence on the golf course, or that desperate need to be a success.

Gary Player

Flory van Donck drives and (inset) Player receives the trophy

1960

THE OPEN

Centenary year, so of course it had to be St Andrews. As the so-called "home of golf" (there are other claimants!) it had always tended to attract a high American entry, but even this and the centenary made no difference in 1960. Just a handful came, but one who did made a world of difference.

That was Arnold Palmer. To achieve a modern Grand Slam was probably his main ambition, for Palmer had brought off the very rare feat of winning both Masters and the US Open, the latter with a charge through the field to take the title with a closing 65. He had become the first golf superstar since the decline of Ben Hogan.

Early on, however, it was the Argentine Roberto de Vicenzo who produced the heroics. His start of 67, 67 had only been bettered by Henry Cotton in 1934. It gave him a seven-stroke lead on everyone except the little fancied, middle-aged Australian Kel Nagle, who lay two behind after a 69, 67 start.

Though no star, Nagle had transformed his game. Once a long hitter with a poor short game, he disappeared, so they say, for a while. When he came back to competitive golf, he was rather short but steady from the tee and a very safe putter.

Meanwhile, how was the superstar doing? His rounds of 70, 71 was good golf, but left him one of a small group those seven strokes behind de Vicenzo.

The Argentine stumbled immediately in his third round with a short putt missed on the 1st. Later, he sent his tee shot through the back of the 338-yard 10th and disastrously took four more to get down. On the long 14th he was out of bounds. His eventual 75 meant the he had thrown away his best chance to-date of winning the championship, but he certainly wasn't out of contention.

The new leader was Nagle, still not much fancied, two ahead of de Vicenzo, with Palmer a couple more in arrears. His 70 could have been a good deal better. Anyone can reckon a 5 on the Road Hole (the 17th) is hardly a failure, but he followed with another bogey 5 on the 18th , one of the easiest final holes in championship golf. It meant Palmer would have to produce a charge to rival his heroics at Cherry Hills a very few weeks before, if he were to win.

And then came the rains. Water cascaded down the clubhouse steps and the greens became unplayable. Play was infact abandoned. Saturday - strange to present-day golf followers - would see the final round.

Palmer, playing just ahead of Nagle, declared his intentions quickly by pitching stone dead at both the 1st and 2nd. Nagle was steadiness itself and made up the lost ground with birdies of his own on the 7th and 8th. De Vicenzo remained well in it until he faded on the second nine. With a birdie to Palmer at the 13th and Nagle later dropping a shot on the 15th, the gap was down to two strokes as Palmer played the 17th - that hole which has so often settled the outcome of great events. Not this time. Palmer gave himself cause for hope by getting his par 4 for the first time all week and then birdied the last. The roar of the crowd came back to Nagle as he settled over a putt of a couple of yards for his own par. He didn't miss and achieved his par on the last with apparent ease to win by a stroke.

Victory had gone to Australia, but Palmer's close pursuit had stirred the senses the most.

Palmer

Kel Nagle

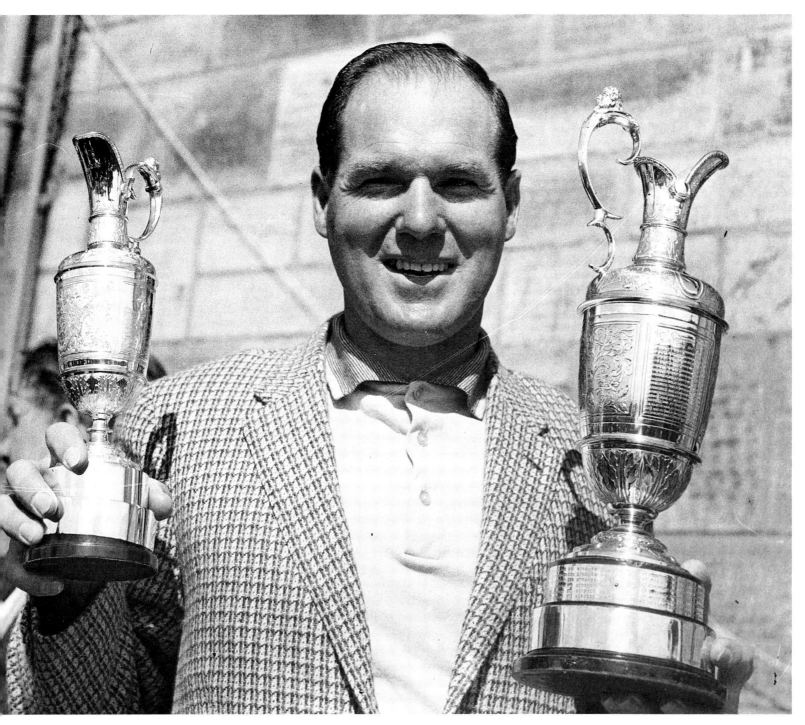

Nagle with the trophy and its centenary year replica

After his first appearance the previous year, most of the talk was about Palmer's chances second time around. His first round left him comfortably placed, a couple of strokes behind Welshman Dai Rees, Kel Nagle and South African Harold Henning – still a success on the US Seniors Tour today.

The weather had been changeable and had a major influence on the scoring. Day Two was very different. There was a tremendous blow which devastated much of the tenting. Of those who qualified for the two rounds of the final day, many managed to get through despite scoring in the high 70s and low 80s.

Palmer played some of the most memorable golf ever seen in the teeth of the very worst of the weather – when he managed to birdie five of the first six holes. No other competitor could lash the ball low under the wind with the long irons as Palmer could. He too, however, had his disasters, particularly on the 16th. Bunkered near the green, his ball moved as he was in mid-stroke – a penalty shot – and the movement also caused him to thin through the green into another bunker. The resulting 7 was only just salvaged.

At the end of the day, the contest already seemed to have narrowed to just four players – Rees and Henning on 142, with Nagle and Palmer a stroke behind. Play was washed out on the Friday, so the final rounds were again postponed until Saturday.

Dai Rees, always likely to begin uncertainly, went two over par on the 1st with a 7. However, the Welshman was a courageous counter-puncher and finished with a 71 – and all this at the age of 48.

Palmer did a great deal better, however, with a 69. He also played the shot of the championship. It is commemorated today with a plaque beside the present 16th (see page 27), one of only two on our championship courses. (The other is on the 17th at Royal Lytham and is a reminder of a long iron from a sandy lie played by Bobby Jones in winning the 1926 Open.)

Playing the 16th (present 17th), Palmer hit a poor drive and was well short in two. His pitch then drifted right on the wind, nearly out of bounds, into dense rough and also at the foot of the famous tenacious Birkdale willow scrub. With no chance of a par, he took

THE OPEN

out his pitching wedge and lashed through both rough and scrub. He got the ball out when most would have taken a penalty drop and what is more, his ball finished right by the hole. What a par 5!

However, should you see that plaque today, just off the 16th fairway, let me tell you there are a couple of mistakes associated with it – quite significant ones. It's on the wrong hole and gives the date as "14th July 1961" – the Friday when play was abandoned and Palmer played cards, not golf.

Palmer increased his lead during the final round to four strokes on Rees with five to play. The Welshman made a brilliant charge at this point, but still came to the last needing a 2 to tie. His 3 was just not quite good enough and Palmer was already moving into golfing legend.

Palmer

Harold Henning

Dai Rees

1962

THE OPEN

Palmer

With his play at Troon, the greatest tournament he ever played, Palmer reached the height of his powers. The final scores give some indication of his achievement: that he won by six strokes is remarkable enough; the gap of 13 strokes before the next men on the prize-money list is truly astonishing.

Yet the condition of the course that year – bone hard and dusty – wasn't well suited to his play. Most of the players were disgusted with it. Good drives to the middle of the fairways sometimes bounded sideways into the rough. It was difficult to accept the course as it was and make the best of good and bad luck alike.

Palmer began with a round of 71, which put him two behind the unknown Keith Macdonald. More significant, though, was Peter Thomson's round of 70 – from the greatest exponent the game has seen of playing a fast-running links course.

His second round 77 put Thomson out of it, however, and Palmer's 69 left him two ahead of Kel Nagle. Paired together with Palmer for round three, Nagle quickly levelled matters and his eventual 70 was a very satisfactory score. Palmer, meanwhile, after an unimpressive start, cut loose. Round in 67, he was five ahead of the Australian and eight ahead of the next man – Bob Charles.

If there were thoughts that the steady Nagle might still do it, Palmer's 33 to the turn in the afternoon banished them and he cruised home to an untroubled 69.

In his two wins he had produced two of the most remarkable spells of dominant golf up to that time. Was there a limit to his powers? It didn't look like it. Yet Palmer was never again to feature as a major force in the Open Championship and in his next two entries finished 26th and 16th.

Peter Thomson

Kel Nagle

Jack Nicklaus makes his Open debut

1963
THE OPEN

The new "golfing phenomenon" holds court with the press

Jack Nicklaus had made his open debut the previous year. Recognised as the new golfing phenomenon and already US Open Champion (his first tournament victory), he had succeeded only in making a thoroughly bad impression. He had finished 34th; had rounds of 80 and 79 amongst his scores, and had run up a 10 on the 11th.

Some said that, with his high shape of shot and his lack of feel in the short game (except for putting), he would never be able to cope with the specialised demands of links golf. They would soon be eating their words.

This year saw the end of what you might call the pre-qualifying tournament over 36 holes. Many had been the times that a pre-championship favourite failed to reach the main event, while others had just managed to struggle through the qualifying and gone on to earn the title of 'the year's champion golfer'. From now on, established players had one test less to endure.

Thomson again made an early mark, getting to the turn in 29 and finishing in the joint lead with the new, flamboyant American Phil

Rodgers. Both kept going the second day with Rodgers leading on 135, Thomson 136 and Nicklaus (71, 67) on 138.

The third round saw no major fluctuations except for a move from New Zealander Bob Charles. With a 66 he broke the Lytham course record and his 206 total gave him a one stroke lead on Thomson, with Nicklaus and Rodgers on 208. The rest, barring a miracle or two in the final round, were no where. So it proved.

Thomson was soon out of the contention, finishing disgusted with a 78 in 5th place, and the main battle was between Rodgers, Charles and Nicklaus.

After 10 holes, Nicklaus took the lead for the first time - but then proceeded to throw the championship away. At the difficult 15th, he hit a superb second shot into the green, but three-putted. Having retrieved that shot with a birdie at the relatively easy 16th, he failed to get down in two from the back of the 17th (I saw him practising the shot from the same place before the 1988 Open began!) and then hit a poor tee shot at the last. Even so, his 70 set the target which Rodgers and Charles had to beat. They came to the last needing a par 4 to win - and many have failed at this hole, caught by the slant of bunkers awaiting the tee shot along the left.

Both holed testing little putts to do so and would return the next morning, a Saturday, to play off over 36 holes.

Perhaps it was then that Bob Charles came to be thought of as the game's best putter. Starting with one across the 3rd green to take the lead, he went on to a total of 11 one-putt greens, a round of 69 and a three-stroke lead.

But it was still all to play for. Despite dropping shots at the first two holes in the afternoon, Rodgers was only a stroke to the bad after the 6th. Thereafter, Rodgers missed green after green and we had the first left-handed winner of this, or indeed any other, major championship. That's still the position today.

The Big Three: Nicklaus, Palmer, Player

Bob Charles with Phil Rodgers

Bob Charles

1964

THE OPEN

Tony Lema

Though few Americans entered for this Open, times were beginning to change. You might say that US tour players who aspired to greatness rather than wealth wanted to win the Open! One who made his first appearance this year was Tony Lema. However it seemed he was just over for the trip, giving himself barely time for a quick practice round before play began in earnest. He would have to rely wholly on his caddie to point the way and select the clubs.

It did him little harm. Enjoying some of the best weather, his 73 placed him just behind the leaders and he followed by easing into a two-stroke lead with a 68 - the best round of the second day. He played just as well on the morning of the final day, with another 68 taking him 7 strokes clear. Was it all over?

The only possible threat seemed to be from Jack Nicklaus. After putting very cautiously and unsuccessfully on the first two days and being rewarded with rounds of 76 and 74, he had decided that come

what may, he would hit his putts firmly at the hole and not try to dribble them in. He was round in 66.

He made a thunderous start to his final round, unbelievably picking up eight strokes on Lema's later scoring for the first six holes. Lema, after his unimpressive start, went on to play brilliantly. He had five 3s in a row, followed by pars and a finish of 3, 4, 4, 3.

The manner of his play impressed St Andrews as much as his five-stroke victory margin. Technically he was not perfection, with a generous loop in his backswing and plenty of body sway. But Lema made it all look the way a golf club ought to be swung and he made it work.

They also highly approved of the way he finished the championship. To the last hole, quite a short par 4, he played the traditional running approach through the Valley of Sin, rather than a high pitch.

Afterwards, Tony Lema followed a precedent he had set after his first US Tour victory - presenting a case of champagne to the press.

Tony Lema

THE OPEN

Despite his consistently brilliant performances during the 1950s, by this time the Australian Peter Thomson had become a figure of the past. He was still recognised as a leading player, except in the USA, with victories continuing elsewhere. But at Open time the talk was far more of such stars as Gary Player, Arnold Palmer, Tony Lema and Jack Nicklaus. Thomson was no longer thought of as a leading contender and certainly wasn't as formidable, apt to produce a poor spell of golf which put him out of the running.

This year he began weakly with a 74, while Tony Lema began his championship defence with all the flair of his play at St Andrews. With a 68 he held the first day lead. He was still there after the second day, though his 72 was bettered by many players, and was joined in the lead by Australian Bruce Devlin, then up and coming but never to make it as a major figure in golf. Thomson had moved up through the field with a fine 68, the best score of the day, and was handily placed two strokes behind the lead.

For the last day there was a far more wind. Thomson now knew he was really in with a chance. I had never seen him appear so coldly determined, the usual smiles banished by concentration.

With his low flight and feel for how the ball would run over the hard ground, Thomson was in his element. Paired with Lema, he went round in 72 to the American's 75. He was in the lead by a stroke from Lema and Devlin, with O'Connor, de Vicenzo and Palmer two behind. Several others still had good chances.

For the final first nine holes, Thomson was steadiness personified, increasing his lead to three. Although he then missed a series of very makeable putts, he was still just ahead of Lema, de Vicenzo and the little Welshman, Brian Huggett, whose closest challenge for the Open this was to prove. He failed because of relatively poor second shots at the last two holes.

These were both par 5s, a little over 500 yards and reachable with two good, but not spectacular, shots. Thomson came to them with a one-stroke advantage on Lema. He needed a couple of 5s to tie others already in the clubhouse, but that was by no means certain to hold Lema at bay.

It was Lema who cracked, finishing 5, 6. Thomson drove securely at both holes and followed with perfectly weighted long irons which pitched well short and then ran on, threading between bunkers to the heart of the two greens. He laid both approach putts close by the hole.... and that was that. At 35 he was the first man since J H Taylor in 1913 to total five Open victories, and he banished thoughts that he had built his great record only because the Americans had lost interest in the Open. The three undisputed giants - Lema, Nicklaus and Palmer - were all at Birkdale, finishing 5th, 12th and 16th respectively.

Palmer

Bruce Devlin - early leader

Thomson watched by Lema (far left)

Brian Huggett

Tony Lema

Thomson

1966

THE OPEN

As the players assembled at Muirfield there was little doubt that Nicklaus, already with three Masters titles under his belt, was the world number one. In the Open itself he had performed well at times and it was the title he now desired the most. This time there were plenty of fellow Americans after it as well, the strongest field so far in modern times.

The course was also the sternest challenge anyone could recall. The rough had been allowed to grow and Doug Sanders was moved to comment that he didn't mind about winning – "I just want the hay concession."

To keep the big hitters in their place, the fairways had been narrowed in their driving area to about 25 yards. Many, Nicklaus included, decided they would play irons from the tee most of the time. As had been done in the US Open, it was decided to restrict players who relied too much on their skills at chipping and little pitch shots. They would seldom be able to make clean contact.

The course was set up to benefit golfers who could place their tee shots on the fairways and hit the greens. Wild power and scrambling looked very unlikely to pay off.

Nicklaus made his best start in the championship to-date. After the first round he was tied with Jimmy Hitchcock on 70 and followed with a 67, in which he used his driver only four times. British pro Peter Butler lay one behind, having broken the course record with a 65. Thereafter, however, he faded right away with an 80.

Phil Rodgers was again making an impression, starting with a 74 and following with a 66. He was three behind Nicklaus, together with South African Harold Henning and Kel Nagle (and how often his name crops up after his triumph in the centenary Open).

In the third round Nicklaus concentrated on safety. For most of the time he kept to par, but shots leaked away over the closing holes and he finished in 75. Rodgers was the new leader on 210. Having reached the turn in 40, he came back in 4, 3, 4, 2, 4, 3, 2, 4 – 30 strokes, which equalled the championship best on any course up to that time.

Nicklaus was two behind on 212, Sanders a stroke further back and Welshman David Thomas, with a 69, was arousing memories of 1958 when he had tied with Peter Thomson before losing a 36-hole play-off. Palmer was on the same score.

Rodgers and Nicklaus were out last on the final day and at the 10th it was over for Rodgers when he recorded a 7 – the same score on the same hole had done for Palmer just minutes before. Nicklaus had reached the turn in 33 and, with no one better than three strokes in arrears, he looked almost home and dry. Almost. He immediately three-putted from about 10 feet just as Thomas holed a huge putt a couple of holes ahead. All to play for once again.

Thomas and Sanders played out their rounds steadily and set a target of 283. Meanwhile, Nicklaus had dropped shots on the 13th and 14th. His lead was gone and he needed to par in to tie. After pars on the 15th and 16th, the 17th – 528 yards with a favourable wind – was a clear birdie opportunity and gave him the chance of outright victory. Where Thomas had failed, Nicklaus did not.

His victory made him only the fourth man to do the Grand Slam of all four majors. He would vastly improve on that record in the years ahead.

Arnold Palmer in the "hay"

Peter Butler (in cap) completes his record-breaking round

Jack Nicklaus

David Thomas

1967

THE OPEN

For years Roberto de Vicenzo had been regarded as the greatest striker in the modern game. Way back in 1948 when Henry Cotton won at Muirfield, he had thought of de Vicenzo as his greatest danger, but Roberto had proved incapable of converting his chances. His tendency to produce the occasional hook had sometimes cost him dear, but putting was far more of a weakness. Once he had missed a tiddler, the heart seemed to go out of him. Despite his several high finishes, no one gave him a chance this year, at the age of 44.

On the other hand, Nicklaus was at the height of his powers and had just added his second US Open, outpacing Palmer in the 18-hole play-off. With Hoylake burned brown, even his high tee shots seemed to run on for ever. Although de Vicenzo, with just a trace of a draw, was perhaps as long.

Because the course was playing short, the first two rounds became something of a putting contest. Many players not thought to have a chance of winning in the cauldron of the last day featured strongly. Of those considered to have a real chance Nicklaus (70, 69) held the second round lead with Devlin – de Vicenzo was on 141.

In the third round the most important scores were the 67s of Gary Player – a second victory overdue – and de Vicenzo. Nicklaus had played very steadily, but had not taken his chances on the greens, impeccable as always at Hoylake. De Vicenzo, on the other hand, was delighted to have found a putting stroke which worked. He went into the final round on 208 – two better than Player and three ahead of Nicklaus – wondering if his putting would hold up, particularly against these two.

There was also the prospect of a charge from Nicklaus. Secure in the knowledge that he was the world's best golfer, he tended to play not to lose – until the final round. Then he was forced to go for everything.

De Vicenzo played the first nine without serious error and Player dropped out of contention early on the homeward nine. Nicklaus was now the only threat to de Vicenzo – if a very substantial one. He drew closer with birdies on the 7th and 8th. There were two par 5s on the second nine where he looked to pick up more strokes –

failing on the 14th, but succeeding on the 16th. With another birdie at the last his round came to 69.

De Vicenzo made the championship virtually his on the 529-yard 16th. Here he played his tee shot close to the practice ground, out of bounds, and then thundered a 3-wood to the heart of the green. Two more superb drives and a couple of 9-irons and he was champion by two strokes.

It was one of the most popular successes of modern times, even more so when Roberto, in his victory speech, hoped that he would be present when a young British player won the title. Two such young men had done extremely well: Clive Clark, now with the BBC golf team, finished joint 3rd; Tony Jacklin was 5th.

The last words should be with Roberto. At a small private party with Royal Liverpool club members afterwards, he clapped one on the shoulder and said: "How about that, amigo? I just come over to see old friends and I win ze bloody championship!"

Player congratulates de Vicenzo

De Vicenzo putts, Player (crouching in black) watches

Clive Clark

Jack Nicklaus

De Vicenzo celebrates

THE OPEN

Carnoustie

Until it was humbled by the still air and draught conditions of 1975, Carnoustie was thought the most daunting course on the Open Championship rota – a reputation enhanced by the fact that Ben Hogan had emerged as champion the last time the event had been played there.

The championship of 1968 did nothing to alter its reputation.

The US contingent continued to be more formidable year by year and 1968 marked the first entry of Billy Casper, just about the most successful tournament player of the times and twice US Open champion.

After a chill and windy first day an amateur, very unusually, held the lead: Michael Bonallack, now secretary of the R & A. Another British player close behind was Tony Jacklin, who had recently amazed everyone by being the first man from this country to win on the US Tour since 1920.

But leading positions this early usually turn out to matter little. It's far more important to note which of the apparent contenders have put themselves *out* of the reckoning. In this instance, Palmer, Thomson, de Vicenzo and Devlin (all 77s), and Sanders (78), seemed to have done just this and also, perhaps, Nicklaus after a 76.

On the second day Casper joined the few who had broken 70 in a Carnoustie Open. With rounds of 72 and 68 he had a four-stroke lead. Nicklaus (69) was back in the thick of it, but ahead of him, on 144, were Bob Charles, the young Brian Barnes, and Jacklin.

In more foul weather, Casper (74) held on to his lead – just. He was a stroke ahead of Charles (on 215) and Player's consistency had paid off, leaving him two off the lead. Nicklaus was four behind Casper.

In the final round Casper and Charles soon began to fade. The main event was the duel between Player and Nicklaus, who made the near fatal error of hooking out of bounds on the par 5 6th, a hole he was looking to birdie. With little hope left, Jack continued to attack but putts wouldn't drop. The real end came on the par 5 14th. He birdied the hole, but Player had already hit one of the truly decisive shots of Open Championship history. He had cracked a blind second with wood over the spectacle bunkers to the heart of the green. Gary knew it was good – but how good? His ball lay just a couple of feet away and an eagle 3 followed.

Player, who didn't have a 6 throughout the championship, eventually got home by two strokes from Nicklaus.

Brian Barnes

Billy Casper

Bob Charles

Jack Nicklaus

1969

THE OPEN

Bob Charles with his first round scorecard

With Peter Townsend, Tony Jacklin continued to look the most likely British prospect for greatness. Both had the ambition to make the prolonged efforts on the US Tour that such members of an earlier generation as Peter Alliss, Christy O'Connor and Dai Rees never attempted. In those days, if you couldn't make it in the United States, there was no way you could hope to be a world beater. How different things are today! The leading Europeans can be satisfied with both the money and the stern competition of their home Tour. Such players as Faldo, Woosnam, Langer, Rafferty and Ballesteros do not care, and do not need, to compete in the obligatory 15 events on the other side of the Atlantic.

Jacklin was having a poor year on the US Tour and had just missed a long sequence of cuts when he arrived at Lytham. Even so, he felt he was in reasonable form.

Any negative thoughts must have been removed by his first round 68, which put him two strokes behind the flying start of Bob Charles. The New Zealander continued with a 69 and would have been well into the lead but for a course record 65 from Christy O'Connor, which brought him up to one behind the leader.

Jacklin, 70, remained well up the field and when he produced another of the same in the third round, with Charles and O'Connor falling away, he had a two-stroke lead over Charles. One stroke further back were de Vicenzo (third round 66) and Thomson.

Jacklin did much to secure the championship with his play on the easier first nine in his final round. With birdies on the 3rd and 4th he opened up a five-stroke gap. After nine he was still four ahead of Charles. It was a very strong position, but one he had to defend dourly.

He did so, keeping Charles at more than arm's length until, on the 17th, he took three putts for the first time in the championship.

Even so, he had a two-stroke lead standing on the last tee. There were still possibilities for a disaster on this very demanding finishing par 4, mainly the rank of bunkers along the left that have trapped so many in championship play over the years.

But Jacklin didn't falter, hitting a vast drive straight down the middle past all the trouble. And that was that, apart from the final formalities. He was the first British champion since Max Faulkner back in 1951.

De Vicenzo

Christy O'Connor

Bob Charles

Jacklin (botto
surrounded b
the Press

One solution to the telephone strike which took place during the 1978 championship!

Peter Alliss 1959

Mr Lu with a spectator previously hit by one of his shots

Past champions line up in 1970
Back row L-R: A G Havers, G Sarazen, R Burton, F Daley, R de Vicenzo,
A Palmer, K Nagle, R Locke, H Cotton, P Thomson
Front row L-R: D Shute, R Charles, M Faulkner, J Nicklaus, A Jacklin, G Player

Lee Trevino...with snake!

Player

A fire on the course – Royal Birkdale 1976

THE OPEN

By the time this Open arrived Jacklin had become a superstar; some were even calling him the greatest player in the world. He had just produced a far greater achievement than his British Open victory by taking the US Open. He was in the lead after every round and, with a very long putt holed on the final green, won by seven strokes. He was the first British winner for fifty years.

Jacklin began the defence of his British title with birdies on the 1st, 2nd, 3rd, 5th, 7th and a 9-iron holed at the 9th for an eagle 2. That was 29 for the outward nine. He continued in much the same vein until he cut his second shot into a bush on the long 14th. Then the skies opened, play was suspended and he had the night to think about what to do next.

The following morning his fires were dampened. With more shots dropped, what seemed likely to be the greatest single round in Open Championship history became 'only' a 67. That, in easy conditions, wasn't even good enough for the lead, taken by Neil Coles with a course record 65. Altogether, nearly 50 players had broken 70 for their first rounds.

This changed drastically on the second day, when only five broke 70. A relatively new name – Lee Trevino, 1968 US Open champion – was in the lead with two 68s. Jacklin and Nicklaus lay a stroke behind.

On the third day there was a stiff breeze. Many couldn't cope and Trevino's par 72 gave him a two-stroke advantage going into the final round over Jacklin and Nicklaus, who had been joined by a pre-qualifier, Doug Sanders.

For some time Nicklaus looked to be the winner, being the only one all day to reach the turn, in strong winds, in 35. He faltered a little coming home, but his 73 set a better target than Trevino (77) or Jacklin (76) managed.

But, in the end, it was a championship for Doug Sanders to win or lose. On the 17th it looked all over, when his second finished in the Road Bunker. Once there, it's difficult enough to get out – to finish close to the hole takes a touch of genius. Sanders had that touch and got out stone dead.

Par to win on the last, with two fairways to drive into and no severe problems with the pitch to the green.

Sanders' missed short putt to win the Open is the most frequently televised piece of golf history of all, but his problems began with a poor pitch which finished towards the back of the green, some 20 yards from the hole. His approach putt was good, but not quite good enough, finishing about 3½ feet away.

Never mind, there was another day to fight. Even so, when asked at the 1990 Open if he still thought about that miss, Doug replied: "Only once a day now."

In the play-off Nicklaus was never headed and steadily increased his lead until it stood at four strokes with five to play. Sanders then launched a spirited counter-attack, reducing the gap to one with two to play. The greatest crisis for Nicklaus quickly followed as Sanders hit and held the 17th green in two. But Nicklaus matched him in finding this fiendishly difficult target.

With the wind following, Sanders tried desperately to reach the green with his tee shot at the last, but came up about 40 yards short of the flag. Nicklaus, needing a birdie to be sure of victory, discarded his sweater and lashed his tee shot through the green – into long grass. It was spectacular, but gave Sanders the easier second shot. He got his run-up to about 4 feet, while Nicklaus's approach died away some 8 feet short. From there, he holed for his second Open title, then caused some consternation by hurling his putter aloft. Sanders became a footnote in golf history. Nicklaus became the first, and still the only, man to win the Masters and the two great Opens twice each.

Neil Coles with his course record score

Lee Trevino practising on the beach

Sanders and that missed putt

Mrs Sanders can't bear to watch

As always, Nicklaus went into this championship favourite. Home money, of course, was on Jacklin and Trevino arrived for his third Open appearance as US champion, having recently defeated Nicklaus in a play-off. He had then gone off and won the Canadian Open, just a notch below full Major status.

Trevino's top form was confirmed by his first round 69 which gave him the lead, shared with Jacklin amongst others. After the second day the two still led, on 130, followed by Liang Huan Lu (quickly dubbed 'Mr Lu') a stroke behind. De Vicenzo and Player were on 141, but the course was playing short and many remained in contention in this close-packed field.

The shape of the championship was defined after the third day. With a 69 Trevino held the outright lead, but Jacklin and Mr Lu were only a stroke behind. No one else was less than three strokes behind these two and none made a strong bid on the last day.

Trevino seized the championship by the scruff immediately in his final round. Holing some good ones indeed, he took only one putt on seven of the first eight greens. Reaching the turn in 31, he had opened a four-stroke gap on Lu and was six better than anyone else.

The championship seemed to be all over and stayed that way until the 17th. Here the famous Trevino fade became a duck hook, high up in the sandhills. His next shot moved the ball just a few feet and his next got him back into play, but into the rough the other side of the fairway. His three-stroke lead over Lu was disappearing. However, on this relatively easy par 5 Lu failed to get his birdie and Trevino's eventual 7 left him still with a vital lead of one on the last tee. He just reached the last green (513 yards in those days) in two and his superb putting touch in this championship enabled him to coast his long putt stone dead.

After Trevino won the US Open in 1968 some thought that because of his very strange technique he might never again win even a run-of-the-mill tournament. The year of 1971 saw him accepted as a great player.

THE OPEN

Lee Trevino

Mr Lu

Jacklin and Trevino

Nicklaus was at it again. He came to Muirfield with both the Masters and US Open under his belt, and therefore a chance of the modern Grand Slam. He was, incidentally, also the holder of the PGA!

Mr Lu quickly put himself out of the championship with an opening 77, but Trevino and Jacklin continued at centre stage, sharing the lead after two rounds, with seven players – including Nicklaus – just a stroke behind.

On the third day Jacklin produced a splendid 67, inside his playing partner Trevino on most greens. Trevino could only manage par after par – until the 14th, the beginning of his amazing finish. First he holed a putt of about 6 yards and then another of as much as a dozen yards on the 15th. Then came an error, as he missed the green at the par 3 16th and found sand. He then thinned his recovery shot which began racing across the green, towards another bunker. However, after bouncing once, it clattered into the flag and dropped into the hole. Much refreshed, he reached the par 5 17th in two and two-putted for a conventional birdie. At the last, he overhit his approach to the rear fringe. It didn't matter. He holed his chip shot.

1972

THE OPEN

Doug Sanders

These dramatics meant that Trevino went into the final day one ahead of Jacklin (207 to 208). Doug Sanders was on 211 and Brian Barnes on 212.

Nicklaus seemed only a distant threat, six behind on 213. He now abandoned his cautious strategy. At last the driver came out of the bag and the birdies mounted up. Reaching the turn in 32, he proceeded to birdie both the 10th and 11th and now actually held the championship lead.

Then the fire and inspiration diminished. In the run-in he dropped only one shot but there were no more birdies. Despite his 66, which equalled the new course record, both Trevino and Jacklin fought to beat his target – but it had been a magnificent failure and ranks with Greg Norman's charge from behind at Troon in 1989.

Doubtless Jacklin and Trevino were much relieved as the roars from Nicklaus's gallery died away. They were having quite a match of their own – mainly exchanging pars with both eagling the 9th.

On the 17th tee they were level. Jacklin drove well, but Trevino hooked into a bunker. He played out then hit his third into rough well short of the green. From there he sent his pitch through the green and partway up a bank. Meanwhile, Jacklin had hit a good second but failed to get his short pitch close. Trevino, however, was muttering that he had thrown the title away. Irritably, he glanced along the line of his chip shot and, almost carelessly, ran it at the hole. Suddenly, his attitude changed – could it possibly be going in! Joy for Trevino and for Jacklin the prospect of the championship lead gone, unless he could hole his medium length putt. He went for it, but his ball finished about 3 feet past and he missed the return.

For a few years, Tony Jacklin had been in constant contention for the title. From 1969 he had produced a sequence of 1st, 5th, 3rd and now 3rd again. Surely, it seemed to many, a second win could not be long delayed? Alas, he was never again to be in real contention.

1973

THE OPEN

Two relatively new American stars were in the limelight as this Troon Open began. Johnny Miller had recently won the US Open from well back with a superb last round 63. Tom Weiskopf was equally a man in form, with a sequence of US Tour victories.

It was the latter who took the first round lead with a 68. Ominously, his closest pursuers were American – Bert Yancey and Jack Nicklaus with 69s and Miller on 70.

The position changed very little after 36 holes, though Weiskopf had increased his lead to three strokes – over Miller and Yancey – with Nicklaus a further stroke away. European players had almost lost touch, the best placed being Christy O'Connor, six off the lead.

A sentimental talking point was the play of the 71-year-old Gene Sarazen on the 8th, or Postage Stamp, hole. On Day One he had holed his tee shot; on Day Two he bunkered it and holed the next. Played twice, putts nil!

To great surprise, Nicklaus disappeared from contention on the third day, finishing nine strokes behind the leader. He showed what he could do when he attacked the course on the final day for a record 65 – much too late.

By this time, however, the contest was virtually between two men: Weiskopf on 206 and Miller a stroke behind. Weiskopf was credited with the most rhythmic, elegant and powerful swing in modern golf but his temperament was suspect. Tom knew his talents were outstanding and the recent death of his father made him resolve not to waste them.

In the final round he played with the greatest composure, quickly increasing his lead over Miller to three strokes and never giving the new superstar cause for hope thereafter. His total of 276 equalled the championship record. After this breakthrough, he seemed destined for more victories in the majors. It didn't happen.

LEADER BOARD

HOLES	PAR	PLAYER	SCORE
72		WEISKOPF	206
72		MILLER	279
72		COLES	279
72		NICKLAUS	280
72		YANCEY	281
72		BUTLER	288
72		O'CONNOR	288
72		WADKINS	288
72		CHARLES	288
72		BARNES	289
72		TREVINO	289

PLAYER | SCORE FOR ROUND

MILLER
WEISKOPF

TROON
GOLF CLUB

Johnny Miller (in cap) with Tom Weiskopf

Jack Nicklaus

1974

THE OPEN

John Morgan - early leader

This was the year the 'big' ball, today's standard, became compulsory in the Open. Before, you could use either size and virtually all competitors chose 1.62 not 1.68.

It had long been argued in Europe that the big ball should become the standard because it was more difficult to control, especially in strong winds. Using it would make players this side of the Atlantic become better shot makers.

Lytham in 1974 was a good test of the theory because the winds were stiff. Many failed, only four players scoring under 290.

Most low rounds on this course are made by birdies on the easier first nine, where there is no really threatening hole. Contrastingly, the 12th, 14th, 15th, 17th and 18th are clear dangers on the second nine.

Gary Player had shown excellent form all year and had won his second Masters. With the tonic of a birdie 2 at the 1st, he reached the turn in 31 and at one time a 67 looked on. However, he dropped two shots at the 17th. Nevertheless, his 69 saw him in the joint lead with John Morgan.

On the second day, Player seized the championship. In strong winds, his 68 put him five ahead of Peter Oosterhuis and Bobby Cole of South Africa, both good performers in the Open at this time. Several made brief challenges to Player's supremacy in the third round and the South African certainly gave them a chance. Even so, despite a 75, he kept a three-stroke advantage on Oosterhuis and four on Nicklaus.

If there was to be a challenge on the final day, it had to come early to unsettle Player. Instead, he had a 2 on the 1st while Oosterhuis took 4. He was out in 32 to 34s from Nicklaus and Oosterhuis. Nicklaus then began to fall away even further and a brilliant finish came far too late. This left Oosterhuis as the South African's only rival over the closing holes. Player was frantic when his second to the difficult 17th found very deep rough and was retrieved only after a long search. His second to the last, which finished through the green against the clubhouse, was a diversion rather than a real danger. He putted it back to the green left-handed and won by four strokes. It increased his tally of majors to eight. Amongst his contemporaries, only Jack Nicklaus had more.

Oosterhuis's second place probably established him as the British Number One, ahead of Tony Jacklin who, on this return to the scene of his 1969 triumph, could manage only 18th place.

Gary Player

Peter Oosterhuis

Gary Player with Oosterhuis

1975

THE OPEN

Feared Carnoustie had its teeth pulled for this championship – the last held here. There was no wind on either the first or second days, and overnight rain between the two meant holding greens on days two and three. On the final day, however, it was a very different story in some wind. Only three players beat the par of 72.

With the greens keen in pace on Day One, no one made Carnoustie's feared reputation look silly. Oosterhuis set an early target with a round of 68. He was followed by a brief comet, Andries Oosthuizen a blond young South African whose performance was his one glimpse of fame, and club professional David Huish from North Berwick.

The long-standing course record of 68, set by Ben Hogan in his winning final round in 1953, was beaten several times on the second day, South African Bobby Cole setting the new one with a 66. Huish followed up his exceptional play of the first day by confounding the experts with an even better score. His 67 gave him the championship lead by two strokes. Could he hold out? The rarified air proved too much for him and he followed with rounds of 76 and 80. However, though an unknown frequently leads a major after one round, Huish's feat over 36 holes was rare indeed.

On the third day, Cole fully maintained his challenge with another 66, to lead on 204, from Newton (round in 65 for 205) and Miller (66 for 206). Next came a man making his first Open championship appearance, Tom Watson on 207. There were several on 208 and, on a closely bunched leader board, many more felt they were still in with a chance.

So far, no one had noticed Watson, but on the final day he was the only man to beat par over the first nine. He then apparently threw his chance away by taking three putts on each of the next three greens. The spotlight switched to Newton. One over after nine, he was two under for the next five. If he could par in, he would be champion.

Meanwhile both Nicklaus and Miller set the target at 280 and Watson continued largely unnoticed. Attention was focused on more likely winners and he came to the final tee needing a birdie to beat Nicklaus and Miller. Although his approach came to rest several yards from the hole, he got it in. His 279 was the score to beat now.

Both Cole and Newton suffered from the meanders of the Barry Burn on the 17th, which crosses the fairway twice, leaving an island of fairway between. With the wind against, no one was trying to clear the second meander, but both these failed to clear the first. Cole mishit his tee shot and Newton mistakenly played a 2-iron when he needed a wood. Playing from the bank, both dropped a shot.

Cole had now to birdie the last to tie Watson, but a 3 for Newton would mean the championship. Both played the hole well but neither got the score they needed.

So, it was to be a play-off over 18 holes between Watson and Newton. The Australian was favourite. He was well known in Europe as a young, tough competitor. Watson was little known this side of the Atlantic, but followers of the US Tour knew he had a reputation as a choker who had faded away after excellent starts in US Opens and had thrown Tour events away with poor final rounds.

However, the result shows that Watson had been tempered by his experiences. After a close contest, his par at the last was good enough for victory by a stroke. A new superstar was on the move. Incidentally, like Lema in 1964, he had arrived late and with no time for a practice round.

Andries Oosthuizen

Bobby Cole

Jack Newton

Tom Watson

Jack Nicklaus

1976

THE OPEN

It's not often you lead a major championship with an 8 on your card, but that's what Irishman Christy O'Connor Junior did. Not regarded as a serious prospect, he was later joined at the top of the leader-board by two unknowns – the Japanese Norio Suzuki and a nineteen-year-old Spaniard called Severiano Ballesteros. They had difficulty in pronouncing his name. They still do. For the record it's 'Bajestayrose'. All had 69s and the young Spaniard thought he might take 80 the next day if the wind got up. With no sort of record behind him, he probably didn't know how good he was.

The next day, Ballesteros scattered a few shots early on, but pulled them back. Again, he finished with a 69 for a two-stroke lead over Johnny Miller.

That quickly went on to the third day when Miller reached the turn with a lead of two strokes, but lost ground as Seve recovered brilliantly after a couple of vast hooks. Suddenly, on the long 17th, he shot into a three-stroke lead with an eagle. A Miller birdie at the last set them back to where they had started, with a two-stroke gap.

Well, Young Tom Morris had won three Opens by the age of nineteen, but those had been very different times. Nothing like this had been seen. Could Seve do it?

The legend was already beginning. The hitting was enormous and, compared with most of the other competitors, usually with the driver. When Seve went into wild country he seemed able to lash the ball out of the worst lies to the green. Around and on the greens his touch and accuracy were phenomenal. Was this a new star or, perhaps, a young man who hadn't learned to fear, playing out of his socks for a few days like Andries Oosthuizen the year before?

In the fourth round, the Birkdale willow scrub gave Ballesteros problems and Miller took the championship lead for the first time at the 6th. He made it his own on the 11th, where he had a 4 to Seve's 7 and then followed up with a birdie and a chip-in eagle. On the leader-board, he was miles ahead, while the young Spaniard was tumbling down.

Miller continued to play impeccable golf and Seve played finely over the last five holes, at the last needing a birdie 4 to tie Nicklaus for second place. After missing the green, he played a deft run-up over humpy ground between two bunkers to secure it. The shot is famous, but actually it was only what he'd been doing all week.

Miller was champion by six strokes with his 66 but, as the future was to show, this was the end of a great few years when he played golf of a quality never clearly excelled.

Ballesteros, having earned just £3,500 in Europe before the Open, finished the season as leading money-winner.

Christy O'Connor Jnr

Ballesteros

Miller

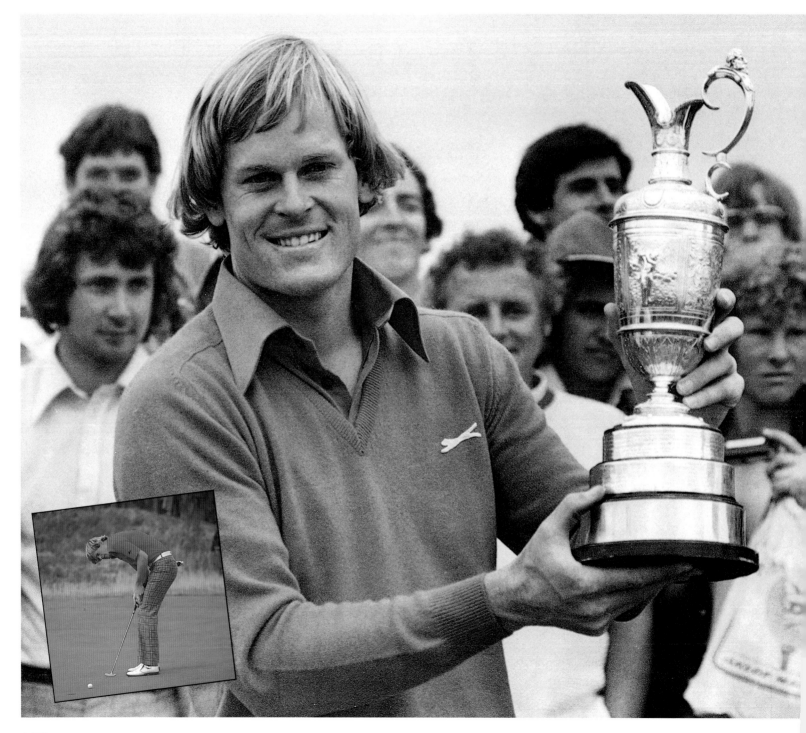

THE OPEN

Turnberry

This year a new course was added to the championship rota for the first time since Birkdale in 1954 – the spectacular Turnberry, on the coast of Ayrshire.

Relatively minor players held the lead after the first and second rounds, but two of the biggest guns – Nicklaus and Watson – were just a stroke behind with identical scores of 68, 70. They were paired for the third round and their superlative play ensured that the pairing would last the rest of the championship.

Both had 65s the third day. They had outdistanced the rest of the field with one exception – Ben Crenshaw. He was still in touch, three strokes behind. No one else was closer than six strokes away.

On the final day, Crenshaw had a bad spell in mid-round and few had eyes for anyone other than Nicklaus and Watson.

In a sense, they were contending for the title of World Number One as well as the championship. Watson had recently won his first

Masters, outplaying Nicklaus over the closing holes, and was also leading money-winner. Over the years Nicklaus had dismissed such rivals for supremacy as Palmer, Player, Weiskopf and Miller. In his late thirties, could he deal with Watson also?

Early on, Nicklaus moved into a three-stroke lead and, despite a Watson counter-attack, still held a narrow one-stroke advantage as they played the short 15th. Here, Nicklaus waited to make his attempt at a birdie putt while Watson prepared to play from short of the green in semi-rough, nearly 30 yards from the hole. Watson holed out to win the hole – yes it was really matchplay by this time.

The championship finally swung Watson's way on the 17th, a par 5 in very comfortable reach for the second shot after a good drive. Watson, playing the shot to the green first, rasped an iron straight over the flag but not close to the hole. Nicklaus's drive had been a huge one, but he was short with his pitch and then ran his ball up 5 or 6 feet past. When he missed that, he had fallen behind at just the wrong moment – only a hole to play.

Watson's play on the last didn't give Nicklaus a glimpse of hope – a 2-iron straight down the middle and a second shot perhaps 2 feet from the hole. Nicklaus did give Watson one final jolt while Tom, it might be said, was thinking out his victory speech. He holed a very long putt for a birdie.

But Watson made no mistake and putted out for his own 3, a round of 65 and what remains the record aggregate of 268, eclipsing the previous 276.

For both players you could say it was their finest hour.

Crenshaw plays watched by Faldo (left)

Nicklaus drives

Watson savours the moment

Nicklaus (far right) walks over to congratulate the victorious Watson

THE OPEN

A repeat of the Turnberry duel was much anticipated as the Open returned to St Andrews, but this was to prove a very different kind of drama. On the first day the Japanese Isao Aoki led the field, the first time a player from that country had done so. He was already well known in this country from his performances in the World Matchplay Championship at Wentworth.

His play is a special delight to those who like to see the unortho-dox. Where Lee Trevino is unusual for his full shots, Aoki makes golf look a very different game whatever he is doing. On the greens, the heel of his centreshaft is set on the turf with the toe on high. In the actual stroke, there's none of the conventional taut left wrist. Instead he gives the ball a wristy jab – and may be the best putter in the world. People seeking a model for their long game should quickly avert the eyes whenever Aoki comes in view. Again, there's the wristy flick and·he's never entirely balanced at any point of the swing. All this is why the experts used to say, earlier in his career, that he was hopeless. But Aoki eventually made it work for him.

On the second day he was still at the top of the leader-board, joined by Ben Crenshaw and Seve Ballesteros. It should have been Ballesteros alone in front, but on the 17th he tried to take a tight line down the right – and went out of bounds.

It was nearly anyone's championship with sixteen players within three strokes of the lead.

There were changes on the third day: Ballesteros, for instance, was out of it with a 76. Another player who took the same total was Tsuneyuki Nakajima, with quite a proportion of that coming at the Road Hole. On the front of the green in 2, he failed to judge the pace and borrow of his first putt and his ball turned towards the gathering Road Bunker, drifting on and on until it toppled in.

Nakajima played shot after shot from the sand, but he couldn't get it right. His intention was to get quick height and clear the bunker wall with hardly any momentum on his ball, so that it died by the hole, set a few yards away. On the fifth attempt he got it right and holed the putt – for a 9.

Tom Watson however, found a way to avoid these problems. After two shots, the Road Bunker lay between him and the flag and he attempted a delicate cut-up shot. Instead he shanked it but, at least, as the ball flew right it avoided the bunker and found the front of the green. At the end he was in the lead, on 211, with the main British hope of the time (though by then resident in the US), Peter Oosterhuis.

The field was still bunched up. A stroke behind came Aoki, Crenshaw, Nicklaus and the New Zealander Simon Owen. Two strokes back were the rising young Nick Faldo, John Schroeder of the US, Tom Weiskopf and Tom Kite, making one of so very many unsuccessful runs at a major championship.

Conditions changed for the final day, with the wind moving from east to north. The story goes that Nicklaus cancelled plans to fly off immediately after the close of the championship – there might be a victory to celebrate. He surmised that many of the field would not adapt to the way each hole would have to be played with different clubs, whereas he had played the Old Course in winds from every quarter.

Owen was paired with Nicklaus, few paying him much attention. He had won a tournament or two but had not been in good form. He was even less noticed after dropping a couple of strokes early on, yet he was, together with his playing partner, to be the main protagonist in the events which decided the championship in the last two hours. Owen began making his move with birdies at the 9th, 10th, 12th and 14th. He then missed the green at the 15th but chipped in for another birdie and the championship lead.

If this was good luck, it was matched by bad luck on the very next hole, the 16th. Here he played a good wedge to the green, but it caught the reverse side of a slope and unkindly skipped and trundled on through the green. A 5 followed, compared with a birdie 3 for Jack. Owen had won and lost the championship lead in minutes.

Nicklaus managed to secure his par on the Road Hole and the last to beat Owen by two strokes.

And what of the overnight leaders? Watson had a bad day, to finish well down the field with a 76, while Oosterhuis came to the 17th with the impossible task of finishing birdie, birdie.

Jack was delighted he'd cancelled his flight plans and duly celebrated his third – and last – Open title.

Simon Owen

Aoki after his four-under par first round

Crenshaw

Kite

Faldo (far left)

Simon Owen

Past champions: Back row L-R: R de Vicenzo, P Thomson, R Charles, A Palmer, J Miller, T Weiskopf, J Nicklaus, R Locke

Front row L-R: M Faulkner, F Daley, A Jacklin, H Cotton, W Muirhead (Capt. of R&A), T Watson, G Player, K Nagle

Bill Longmuir still plays the European Tour with moderate success – he's never won on it but he has won elsewhere, mostly on the Safari Tour. He had *great* success on the first day at Lytham in 1979. He played the outward nine in 29 strokes and held his round together the rest of the way. With a 65 he had played a record-equalling first round and it was only the fourth time that nine holes had been covered in 29 strokes. He led by three from Hale Irwin, recently crowned US Open champion for the second time.

Longmuir didn't play badly the second day and still held 3rd place after a 74. The most likely looking winner, however, was Irwin, who had added a second 68. But the story of the day was the round of Seve Ballesteros.

As mentioned earlier, the first nine at Lytham don't present severe difficulties. The holes are often also wind-assisted, the reverse being the case on the second nine. Seve got to the turn in 33, which on paper looks a better score than it actually is. Thirty-six back, however, is better golf because of the difficulty of the closing stretch. Over those last five holes, all of them par 4s, most players would be content with an average of four-and-a-half. Seve came in 3, 3, 4, 3, 3 – a supreme spell of golf for a round of 65. After an opening 73, he'd shot up the field to second place behind Irwin, with whom he was to be paired for the remainder of the championship.

Day Three was windy and saw highly contrasting play from the two leaders. Irwin, the master technician, got distance and accuracy in his long game, but putted only steadily. Ballesteros missed most of the fairways and many greens, but his short game was at a peak. If he was in a greenside bunker, he inevitably got down in two from there. It must have been wearing on Irwin's nerve, but at the end of the day he still retained his two-stroke lead, both getting round in 75.

That lead went in the first minutes of the final round, with Ballesteros beginning 2, 4 and Irwin 3, 6. Some of the rest of Ballesteros's round is worth highlighting. The shape of the 486-yard 6th favours a draw – Seve hooked his ball across the neighbouring 14th fairway. From there neither he nor his caddie had much idea of the yardage to the green and he hit his second a long way through. Even so, he went on to par the hole.

The 13th saw him at his most attacking. It's a short 4 of 339 yards, but his ball tumbled into a bunker. His splash out was relatively poor, only finishing on the fringe of the green – but he then chipped in.

Others, if not Irwin, were still in close contention for the championship, but Seve scented his first major. As one by one the challengers fell away, he was at times rushing to play his next shot.

His finish was typical of his play. On the 16th he hit his tee shot into an area along the right reserved for BBC vehicles (which earned him the title 'car park champion' in the USA), but still got this birdie 3. Bunkered beside the 17th green, he inevitably got down in two more and at the last again missed the fairway by miles – on the left this time – but moved on smoothly to his 70 (the lowest round from anyone who mattered) and a three-stroke victory.

Bill Longmuir

Irwin congratulates Ballesteros

1980

THE OPEN

Although Tom Watson had taken the championship twice in the previous five years, his performances overall had been patchy. At Lytham the previous year he had finished unimpressively (76, 81), and at Birkdale in 1976 he missed the cut.

This year, however, he threatened his all-time record aggregate of the 1977 Turnberry Open and it was nearly all over by the end of the third day.

After Day One Watson led alongside a revived Lee Trevino, after 68s from both of them. Trevino played just as well the second day and with a 67 was three ahead of Watson, Ken Brown and Jerry Pate. The championship at feared Muirfield showed some remarkable scoring. The unknown Horacio Carbonetti scored a course record 64 on the second day, while Isao Aoki broke that the third day with a 63, equalling Mark Hayes's championship record 63 at Turnberry in 1977.

These rounds no doubt delighted them both. They had no significance to the outcome of the championship, however, although there was a 64 the third day which undoubtedly did. Including a homeward nine in 30, it came from Watson and, with Trevino

fading to a 71, it gave him a four-stroke lead. Brown joined Trevino in second place.

Though there was hope that the British player might pull it off, Ken himself expressed little confidence. He took 76. No one else threatened Tom and with the difficult task of protecting his lead, he never looked in the least likely to throw it away. With a 69 he had his third championship in only six entries.

In contrast to recent years the Americans looked as formidable as ever, taking the first three places and 8 of the top 10.

Trevino

Ken Brown

Aoki and his record scorecard

Watson on his way

1981

THE OPEN

The championship had not been held in Sandwich at Royal St George's since Bobby Locke won his first title in 1949. There had been the feeling that the course included too many blind shots and that road access was extremely poor. In the intervening years, changes had brought improvements in both these respects and no doubt the R&A felt that using a course in the south of England balanced the total bias towards the north-west coast of England, and Scotland.

For once the main story of the first day's play was not about the leaders (the little-fancied Nick Job and Vicente Fernandez, both on 70). Instead, Jack Nicklaus dominated the headlines because of his horrendous total of 83. He reached the turn in 39 and then produced four double-bogeys in a run of 6, 5, 6, 5, 7. Though he then pulled himself together, it was his worst round of golf since he had turned professional twenty years before.

In better weather the following day, Nicklaus hit back splendidly. With no apparent chance of beating the 36-hole cut, his 66 enabled him to do just that. By this time, with a 66 of his own, the American Bill Rogers was in a narrow lead of one stroke on 138, over Ben Crenshaw and Nick Job.

Rogers was equally successful the third day, when his 67 gave him the almost invincible lead of five strokes over Bernhard Langer and Mark James.

Rogers had not been fancied before the championship began, but he was in fact at the peak of what was to prove a very short career at the top. In Britain he was mainly known for having won the World Matchplay Championship at Wentworth in 1979. Before 1981 he had only one US Tour victory, but had won another in the spring and later tied for 2nd place in the US Open.

These were his none too impressive credentials before the Open, but Rogers enjoyed a magnificent year and by the end of it had the best record of anyone.

Despite his lead, he looked vulnerable when he played the par 5 7th badly in 7, allowing Langer to get within a stroke. However, he quickly recovered the lost ground with birdies on the 9th and 10th and encountered only one more obstacle. With a four-stroke lead playing the last, as the crowds surged around him, Rogers was stopped by a policeman. He was able to explain that he was not an unruly spectator trying to push his way through, but the man about to become Open Champion!

Mark James

Ben Crenshaw

Bernhand Langer

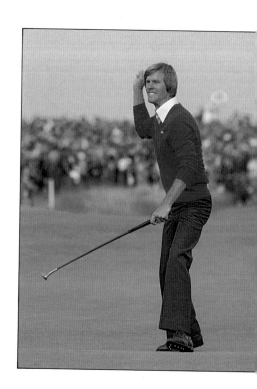

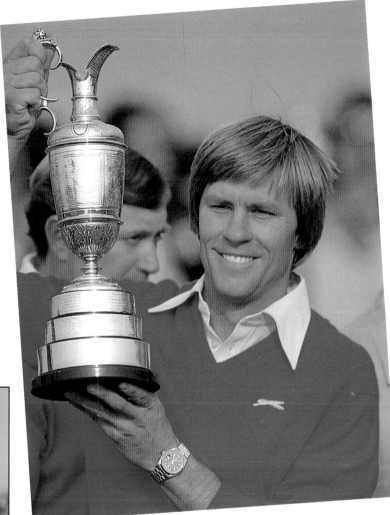

Andy Bean

Johnny Miller

Nick Price

2
8
9
1

THE OPEN

This year the early leader was far more of an unknown than Bill Rogers – the 22-year-old American Bobby Clampett. He was without a win on the US Tour, but an excellent money-winning year in 1981 had marked him out as perhaps the pick of the latest crop of young players.

Clampett began with scoring not seen at the Open since Henry Cotton's 1934 start of 67, 65. As a result of splendid iron play and an excellent short game, Clampett came close to this pace, taking the lead by two strokes after a first round 67. His 66 on the second day put him five ahead of the second place man, Nick Price. Six others were already between six and eight strokes further away. Clampett didn't seem to be an unknown enjoying a brief spell in the limelight. It was more likely we were seeing the arrival of a new star – like Seve Ballesteros in 1976.

Though he dropped a stroke on the 1st hole on Day Three, Clampett increased his lead over the closest pursuer to seven strokes after birdies on the 4th and 5th. Then came disaster at the 6th. He went from bunker to bunker and in the end an 8 went down on his card. Even so, he still held a five-stroke lead.

But the carefree confidence was fatally eroded. There were no major setbacks for the rest of his round, but shots leaked away and he finished with a 78, his lead now a single stroke over Price.

Bobby Clampett was very soon gone the final afternoon. With a three-stroke swing in Price's favour on the very first two holes, the young American was finished. In the years that followed he did not become a star and we can only wonder how his life would have changed had he been able to maintain his early momentum through-out the championship.

On the final day, in a close-packed field many had their chances, none more so than Price. Wth a run of birdies on the 10th, 11th and 12th he was three ahead. Tom Watson, the only championship winner amongst those in real contention, was trying to make a move and did so on the 11th with a superb iron to the flag and an eagle putt.

He made no further move but played steadily to the finish, drop-ping only one shot. Price then had 'only' to hold his game together to win. He took 6 on the 15th, a par 4, and dropped another on the difficult 17th, a long par 3. Watson felt he hadn't *won* the champi-onship, but it went down on his record all the same.

Bobby Clampett

Nick Price

144

Tom Watson

1983

THE OPEN

Before play began this year the players, with almost a single voice, bewailed the condition of the course. Good weather for grass meant that the rough was not only long but – far more important – dense. Once in there, you had to abandon thoughts of going for the green and take your medicine, wedging your ball back into play. The ball also settled down close to the greens, making chipping and little pitch shots more a matter of hope, with clean ball-contact impossible.

What we actually saw during this championship, however, was the lowest scoring ever from the high placed competitors. Why did this happen? It was the condition of the greens that caused it. They putted extremely truly and were also holding – some called them far too soft for an Open Championship links. Whatever the terrors of a course, modern tournament professionals inevitably score low when the greens favour target golf and putt truly.

This was a time when an American winner was still expected – Tom Watson perhaps the obvious choice. However, after the achievements of Ballesteros in the US Masters (he had taken his second title earlier this year and made an excellent run at the US Open), such a result was no longer a foregone conclusion. Many thought him the world's best player. The main British hope was Nick Faldo. He had played consistently well in the Open for several years and was the man in form, having taken three successive European Tour events.

Faldo's start was disastrous. He dropped a couple of shots at each of the first two holes. Was it a portent for the days to come that for the rest of his round he was seven under par, finishing with a 68? This was a courageous come-back indeed.

Ballesteros, on the other hand, spoiled a steady opening round with a 6 on the last for a 71. In a low-scoring championship, this was to prove too much of a burden.

One man who made more headlines was Bill Rogers. Holes-in-one may cause gasps of amazement but they are by no means rare. Rogers transcended such everyday stuff with an albatross 2 on the par 5 17th. It meant a round of 67 and joint second place with Tom Watson and Bernhard Langer.

Craig Stadler, aided by a charmed putter, was round in 64 – which might have been even better. He hit some poor shots on the last two holes when a 62 looked in sight.

It was obvious that everyone would have to attack even to stay in contention this year. Trevino early added a 66 to his opening 69, including an outward nine in 30. The unregarded Denis Durnian eclipsed even this kind of scoring with an outward 28 – a new record.

At the end of the day Stadler had just held on to his lead – one stroke ahead of Watson and Trevino on 135 with Faldo, after another 68, on 136 and Hale Irwin 137. Thirteen more players were within six shots of the leader.

The field continued to be close-packed at the end of the third day, but the scoring was not quite as low. Watson's 70 was enough to give him the outright lead on 205, followed by Stadler a stroke behind and Faldo, Floyd and Graham on 207. Trevino, too, was still there on 208 and four more followed on 209. All ten were credible contenders, but one of them – Irwin – must have been rueful. Needing a casual tap-in for his par on the 14th he had been a little too casual and played an air shot.

In the pressure of the final day some of the contenders faded away – Stadler, Floyd and Graham all taking 75s. The early target was set by a man well out of the running who finished his round of 64 hours before the leaders were home. He was the Australian Graham Marsh.

As the day unfolded, Faldo for some time had a good chance of becoming the first British winner since Tony Jacklin, but faded. Though it seemed to me that it was his putting which let him down on this occasion, Faldo himself did not fully trust his swing. His wilderness years followed directly on from this.

Eventually Andy Bean and Irwin, with last round 67s apiece, set the new target, one lower than Marsh. With the other contenders out of it, the championship was left to Tom Watson to win or lose. As at Troon in 1982, he made a move on the 11th with a birdie after being two over par on the outward nine. Another followed on the 13th and then a saving, twirling putt for par on the 14th. The 16th, where he holed from several yards for another birdie, gave him the chance of a 5, 4 finish (two pars) for the championship.

Despite a big hook from the tee on the 17th, he still managed a par and then faced the very testing final hole – 473 yards of it. Tom's drive was banged down the middle and his long iron into a left-to-right wind was the equal of Ben Hogan's to the final green at Merion in the 1950 US Open. A comfortable two putts later and he was champion for the 5th time in nine entries. Harry Vardon's all-time record of six victories seemed at his mercy. He was 33 years old.

Craig Stadler

Denis Durnian

Lee Trevino

Hale Irwin

Graham Marsh

1984

THE OPEN

History may show that the most significant happening at St Andrews this year was that Tom Watson just failed to equal Vardon's record and never came quite as close again (not even at Troon in 1989).

This was a championship when unknowns made strong moves, but faded. Bill Longmuir (remember him from 1979?) was one of these and he tied for the lead at the end of the first day with Greg Norman and Peter Jacobsen.

The second day belonged to Australian Ian Baker-Finch. He had done very well before he even teed off, with a 68 on Day One, and was six under par for the day after he had played ten holes. Baker-Finch then parred his way home for a 66, the round of the day and the championship lead by three strokes. Were we seeing the arrival of a new star or a brief comet?

The third day made the championship into a four-horse race. Baker-Finch played good golf for a 71, but Tom Watson made the going. Apart from a dropped shot on the 2nd, his golf was almost flawless. With a sprinkling of birdies he got to the turn in 32 and picked up two more almost immediately on the 10th and 12th. Like Baker-Finch the previous day, he parred his way in – even coping with the dread 17th this time. Having taken a 5 and a 6 in his earlier rounds, Watson was content to aim for the front of the green and was rewarded with a two-putt par. He finished in 66 and a total of 205, the same as Baker-Finch. Close behind came Bernhard Langer and Seve Ballesteros on 207. The next men, on 212, were surely out of it unless one of them could produce a 65. No one did and the championship was fought out as predicted – but as a three-horse race, not four.

Baker-Finch quickly dropped out. On the 1st he was a little unlucky when his approach shot spun back into the Swilcan Burn, although thereafter he dropped shot after shot with less excuse.

Langer and Watson also began their rounds unsteadily while Ballesteros – some might say uncharacteristically – continued on to pile par upon par as he had done in earlier rounds. From the tee, his aim was to avoid fairway bunkers and he didn't much mind where he aimed to make this more likely. Conventional wisdom for playing St Andrews is that you can usually go well left and avoid trouble, but that second shots are almost always easier from as near the right edge of the fairway as you dare. Ballesteros was accepting the limitations of his policy. Perhaps as a result, he wasn't often getting his approaches near the hole. Well though he then seemed to be putting, nothing was dropping for him.

A crisis came for Watson on the very easy 12th hole, only just over 300 yards. Instead of a birdie, he dropped a shot by driving into gorse and taking a penalty drop. It cost him the lead, yet he hit back moments later with a birdie on the 13th, while Seve birdied the long 14th. This left Langer two behind the leaders but not out of it. The championship was likely to turn on how the leaders played the 17th.

First came Ballesteros, (playing with Langer ahead of Watson and Baker-Finch) with three 5s on the hole so far out of only four bogeys in his first three rounds. His drive was in the left rough. A 5 was easy enough to get but he had little or no chance of holding the narrow green, which lay at an angle to his line of approach.

But that is exactly what Ballesteros did, two-putting for his par. As he left the green, he was aware that Tom had played an ideal tee shot tight down the right-hand side of the fairway and close to the out of bounds. From there he had a relatively easy second shot. Surely there would be a play-off unless one of them birdied the last?

Watson now made two fatal errors: one was in club selection, choosing a 2-iron when a 4 would almost certainly have been enough; the other was in his execution of the shot itself. Trying to draw the ball into the flag, he pushed it – and finished only a foot or so away from the stone wall over the road that runs along the right side of the green.

Ahead, Ballesteros knew none of this. Mentally he had conceded Watson a par 4. He would need to birdie the last to be sure of a tie for the championship. His drive and approach were good and his putt excellent for strength but not direction. It always looked likely to miss on the right, but instead it died on the right lip and toppled in. The Spaniard was impassioned. Now he was sure to tie. In fact it was all over – he'd won.

Ian Baker-Finch

Baker-Finch

Langer

Greg Norman

Ballesteros with Harry Carpenter

1985

THE OPEN

If the 1984 St Andrews Open will go down in golf history because of its great climax, Sandy Lyle's won't. However, at Sandwich he became the first British winner of the championship since Jacklin's victory at Lytham in 1969, and that's real history. His win was also a very significant part of the revival of British golf and the consolidation of the European Tour.

But, to begin at the end, Sandy's final moments weren't glorious. The 18th at Royal St George's is both difficult and unfair. If I were playing it I'd try to hit a drive down the left side of the fairway and play a runner, going a bit left to right, to the green. I would almost certainly fail and most championship contenders also fail at this hole. Hitting the ball further than I do, they still have the problem of playing a long iron to a green designed to receive a high pitch (when the hole was played as a par 5).

Lyle, however, hit a big drive and was left with a 6-iron second shot. This wasn't bad, but he came down on the left side of the green – without that left to right movement on his ball – and his shot fell away into quite thick greenside rough. From there he played a bump shot into the slope in front of him and didn't hit it quite firmly enough. His ball came back almost to his feet. Despair.

This was certainly anti-climactic, but eventually he became the champion. Let's see how things went earlier.

The star of the first day was Christy O'Connor, with no par on his card until the 11th. Before, there'd been a mixture of birdies and bogeys but he was 30 to the turn. With less dramatic golf on the second nine, he came in with a 64 and a four-stroke lead. Two people who were later to matter, Lyle and the Australian David Graham, were amongst five with 68s. The overwhelming favourite, Ballesteros, took 75.

Then very bleak weather struck. Jack Nicklaus missed the cut. O'Connor subsided to a 76 which could well have been much worse. Bernhard Langer played magnificently for a 69. Lyle dropped two shots on the opening hole but, the man to back in foul weather, compiled a 71 which tied him for the lead with Graham.

The third day gave the leaders better weather than those out earlier. At times, Lyle looked to be drifting out of it, but managed to play a little pitch dead at the 17th and hole a brave putt on the last.

Even so, he was three behind Langer and Graham. It seemed just about the right time for Langer, the year's Masters champion and with two second places in the Open, to win.

On the last day Tom Kite forged through, for a while, but fell away with a 6 on the par 4 10th. Behind, Lyle was playing steadily. Others were not – including Langer with a flurry of 5s on the opening holes. Graham was just as lacklustre, dropping shots to par three times in the first five holes.

Well ahead, Payne Stewart was in the clubhouse with the equal lowest round of the day, a 68, setting an overall target of 283.

Several ought to beat it – only Sandy Lyle did. As time rolled on it looked as if anyone who made a move might be champion. Lyle's move came at the 14th when he had a 200-yard *third* shot to the green and then holed out from off the green. The next he birdied. Suddenly, he needed par over the last three to be virtually certain of victory.

Sandy didn't do it, but he forced in 4-footers at the 16th and 17th for pars.

Then the last. There was that misjudged or mis-struck little shot, but he might still win if he could get down in two more. His fourth was good and left him a two-and-a-half foot putt for his bogey 5. Into the middle it went. Stewart was beaten. What could the last pair out, Graham and Langer, do?

At the 18th both needed birdies to tie and both bogeyed the hole. It was Lyle's championship.

David Graham

Ballesteros

Langer emerges from taking shelter from the rain

Payne Stewart

Although only Tom Watson and Jack Nicklaus had scored sensationally low in the 1977 Open Championship here, the R&A had toughened it for this year. The rough was long and dense and the fairways narrow. Some players, Ballesteros in particular, complained they were trying to make it too much like a layout for the US Open, where extremes of weather are not common.

And extreme was hardly the word for the weather at Turnberry. The opening day was foul, with the kind of biting winds that put the most confident and rhythmical swings out of kilter. Only players in excellent form would survive the test.

One such form horse was the 4-1 favourite, Seve Ballesteros – fresh from four consecutive wins and with almost twice as much prize-money as anyone else on the European Tour. The leading US money-winner was Greg Norman, although his had been a disappointing season. He had led both the Masters and the US Open going into the last round, but not held on in either.

At the end of the day, only one player had matched par, Ian Woosnam, who had the unique distinction of being the only man in the field to birdie the 440-yard 14th. He rasped in a 1-iron to do so while many declared they were well short with two drivers. It was, said Ian, the best 1-iron he had ever hit!

Close behind on 71 were Nick Faldo, Gordon J Brand, Robert Lee and Anders Forsbrand. Some were already gone, including the year's Masters champion (Nicklaus), the current US Open champion (Ray Floyd), and the title holder (Sandy Lyle). Each had a 78.

But Turnberry did have a weakness in its defences. The greens were holding and scores improved drastically in lower winds. Ian Baker-Finch, for example, improved to 69 after an initial 86.

Norman's improvement was far more significant, however. On the first day he struggled to what was, in the conditions, a good 74, but he now equalled the Open Championship record with a 63. Containing eight birdies and an eagle it was perhaps just as remarkable for including 3 bogeys, one coming from a three-putt on the last green.

His round gave him the lead by two from Gordon J Brand, with

THE OPEN

Tsuneyuki Nakajima a couple further away with Faldo. Nakajima's 67 was notable for including 12 single-putt greens. He kept going well on the third day, when the leaders had to contend with lashing rain late in the afternoon, for a 71 and a total of 212, one behind Norman.

The Australian had looked to be taking charge of the championship at one point, being five ahead of the field, but dropped strokes later meant a 74. At the end of the day his closest pursuers were Brand and Woosnam, three behind.

Going into the final day, which was sunny with the wind dropping away, Norman's temperament was much in question. He was a superstar on every continent but had won no major championship.

In the event, no one put him under much pressure and he played finely for a 69. A tremendous boost for his hopes came on the very first hole: he parred; Nakajima took 6, missing a putt of about a foot. On the 3rd Norman was bunkered more than 20 yards from the flag – and holed out for a birdie. He was five strokes in the lead. There would have to be sensational play up ahead or Norman would have to play badly indeed to lose that kind of lead.

Norman himself didn't feel that the title was his until quite some time later when, on the 8th, he cracked a 4-iron close and holed the putt. Perhaps the only real alarm came on the 17th. Faced with a putt of 3 – 4 feet, he told his caddie he couldn't even see the hole. This was borne out by his shot, which didn't touch the hole and went at least 3 feet past. However, he got that one in and the rest was a triumphal progress to a five-stroke victory.

Norman, he himself said, had got the monkey off his back. Full of confidence he went off to the US PGA, led after every round and went into the last one with a four-stroke lead – only to subside to a 76 and eventual defeat when Bob Tway holed out from a greenside bunker on the last. Norman has won no majors since his momentous 1986, when he led every one of them.

Gordon J Brand

Ballesteros

Tommy Nakajima

1988

THE OPEN

Rodger Davis

This time the form horse was Ian Woosnam, fresh from the Scottish Open at Gleneagles and rounds of 65, 65, 66, 68 for a seven-stroke win, his third of the season.

But Australian Rodger Davis made the most headlines the first day with a 64 (which, incidentally, left Woosnam seven behind). He had certainly made the good start which was thought essential in the easy conditions. Trevino, Ken Green and Bob Tway followed on 67, while Paul Azinger (current leading money-winner in the US Tour), Larry Mize, Nick Price and Nick Faldo all had 68s.

The saddest story of the second day was the fate of Arnold Palmer. Standing on the 14th tee at level par for his round, he drove into a fairway bunker, just got out but then struck a long iron into a greenside bunker. This time, it cost him five attempts to escape. He ended up with a 10 on his card, his first double figures for a hole in a major championship. Commented Palmer wryly: "Perhaps God could have got it out of there, but he'd have had to have thrown it!"

Paul Azinger

Azinger, after a second round 68, was the new leader with Faldo, Australian Gerry Taylor, Davis and Payne Stewart one behind. The field was very bunched up, fourteen being within three shots of the leader.

The weather on the third day changed all this. It was cold, wet and windy, especially for the earlier starters. Scores in the high 70s and low 80s were frequent. Gary Player felt that his 79 was only about four worse than par for the day.

Later the rain stopped and the wind dropped, but there were no scores lower than 70 and the round of the day was Sandy Lyle's 71, in the worst of the weather. Azinger clung on to his lead in his first Open by one from David Frost of South Africa, with Faldo, Craig Stadler, Tom Watson and Payne Stewart only two off. No doubt there were several others who considered themselves in with a chance – if they could shoot a 66.

No one did and the day's low round was a 67 from David Feherty – but it came after a 77. Of those still contending, the lowest score came from Ben Crenshaw, whose 68 eventually brought him into a tie for 4th.

For a long time it looked to be Azinger's championship. His 34 to the turn was not bettered by anyone and he increased his lead to three strokes at this point. He then bogeyed both the 10th and 11th and failed to make the most of birdie chances at the 12th and 14th. They would have put him almost out of sight, but he still held a one-stroke lead with the par 5 17th and the very difficult 18th to come.

But let's consider Faldo's round. Basically it was par all the way with some birdie chances he couldn't convert early on. He also saved pars with some excellent play from greenside bunkers.

He looked at no scoreboards, but as he played the 18th it seemed likely this Open would see a play-off. Faldo hit a good tee shot up the fairway and followed with an iron bang on line, but which pulled up perhaps a dozen yards short of the flag. His approach putt was too firm, running about three-and-a-half feet past. But he got it down and had set the target for Azinger to beat.

The American made fatal mistakes on the last two holes and finished 6, 5. Faldo was a champion and a multi-millionaire of the immediate future.

Nick Faldo

Fuzzy Zoeller and Arnold Palmer

Woosnam with his caddie

THE OPEN

Seve Ballesteros had been having a quiet time in the Open (though there was a last round 64 at Turnberry), but he started with verve this year. Birdying five of the first seven holes, he reached the turn in 30 – which was something of an anti-climax considering his first three holes. His opening iron shot to the par 3 1st came to rest a couple of feet away. The same thing followed at the 2nd. At the 3rd, however, he wasn't quite as close – about five yards away – but that putt went in as well!

When a great player starts like that, he may find himself thinking: "This is my championship." But there were still 69 holes to play.

As regards the rest of his first round 67, it is probably bushes rather than birdies which will go down into golfing legend. On the day, the 445-yard 14th played as a par 5 and this is where Seve got his 'bogey'. From the tee he hooked into rough but, fired up, decided to go for the green with a long iron, snap-hooking into bushes instead. The ball was found and he went back some 40 yards before taking his penalty drop. Then he got down with an iron and single putt from about 5 yards.

At the next hole he hit a short drive and couldn't reach the green with his second, but pitched and one-putted for his par. The 17th he birdied from 2 feet and then at the last hit his drive into bushes along the right. Again he had to drop out under penalty, was just short of the green with his third but got down in two more.

In difficult winds these heroics gave him a two-stroke lead and reminded him that this was the course where he had won before, in 1979.

The second round saw the championship take its final shape. Ballesteros (71) kept his confidence intact. He was, however, overtaken by Nick Price, of Zimbabwean upbringing and the man who had "thrown away" the 1982 Troon Open. In friendlier weather, he had a 67 to lead from Seve by one. The defending champion Faldo then followed two further behind, with Craig Stadler making another spirited assault on the Open which, again, was to come to nothing.

The third day was rained off after nearly half the field had begun their rounds. This must have vastly pleased one player – Brian Marchbank – who had dropped five strokes in seven holes. Veteran American Hubert Green, on the other hand, was five under for the same stretch, but was able to say: "It's not the end of the world."

After the deluge it was at least possible that the championship could be rained off. But links courses, with their sandy base, drain well if the rain stops. Eventually it did. Before, there had been planning for a 36-hole finish on the normal last day (Sunday) until it seemed that there might not even be a course playable for one round.

But it *was* possible to play the third round that day. Price (69) kept a lead of two on Ballesteros, who had a 70 which included two left-handed shots from beneath bushes. A 68 from Faldo brought him up into a tie for 2nd. Sandy Lyle, the Masters champion and leading US money-winner, came into the picture with a 67 to be three behind Price's 206 total.

The scene was set. No one else had a realistic chance at six or more behind.

On the final day, the last threesome of Price, Faldo and Ballesteros were centre stage, except when Lyle made a brief spurt.

This was indeed a matchplay finish no less dramatic than Turnberry in 1977. Seve made the most emphatic start with a birdie chance from about 7 feet which he missed. On the 2nd he missed another, but Price dropped a shot to be only one in front and then looked fragile when he needed a long putt to save his par on the next hole.

Well ahead, Fred Couples had consecutive eagles on the 6th and 7th, seeming to put himself in real contention. This was not so, because Ballesteros and Price were about to embark on some great scoring feats. Lyle also looked promising at about this point, though he too faded.

The 7th put paid to Faldo. On this par 5 he hit a good second shot, but it left him having to judge the pace and line of a putt which had to swing up and down a greenside bank. He was too weak. Only a par, to remain at 6 under. His companions both birdied.

On the next hole Seve levelled what was to be a match between two players the rest of the way, with a birdie. On the 11th he took the lead for the first time since the second day with another birdie, from about 7 yards. He lost it by dropping a shot on the next hole.

The 13th must have been sickening for Price. He almost holed his second shot, but Ballesteros matched that birdie from about 4 yards. On the 16th Seve put his second shot stone dead to take the lead again.

It still all depended on the difficult final hole. In two Price was on but with no realistic chance of a birdie. Seve, from well off the green, his ball half covered by grass, played the chip of a lifetime. It didn't go in but, perfect in pace, touched the hole and stopped a very very few inches past.

He wasn't quite champion – Price could still tie from about a dozen yards. But it just wasn't at all likely. He charged at the hole and missed the return, which by then didn't matter in the least.

Ballesteros with Price

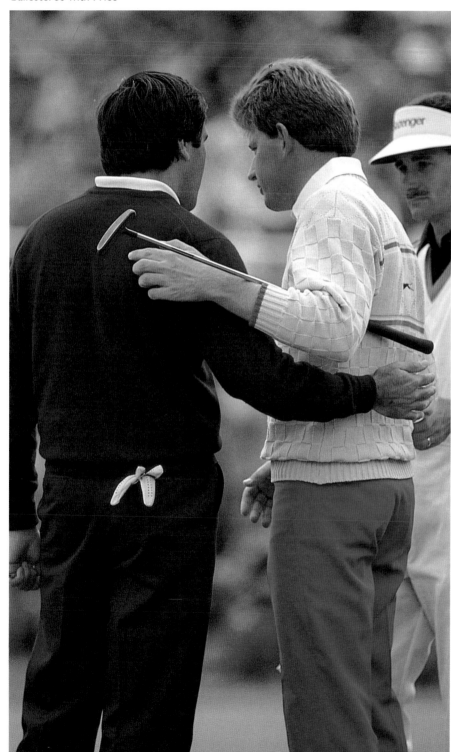

Price and (inset) Stadler

Faldo

1989

THE OPEN

After nasty weather in the Open for a few years, we now had heat and a very different kind of contest. Ballesteros had won his Open against a last round performance from Price that would itself usually have won. At Troon, Greg Norman was in a near hopeless position, yet so nearly won outright with one of the great charges of championship history.

As it was, this championship saw the first-ever threeway play-off (between Norman, Mark Calcavecchia and Wayne Grady) and the first trial of the R&A's compromise between sudden death and the traditional 18-holes.

And what a play-off it was! The inspired Norman, despite having to wait around a couple of hours, found the fire still there. He began with a brace of birdies to be '2 up' on fellow Australian Grady, but only one on Calcavecchia. A dropped shot on the difficult par 3 17th had the pair level.

So it was all on the last once more – unless they had to carry on after a tie.

Calcavecchia hit a rather poor tee shot into the right rough, but into a good lie. Norman then rasped away the drive of the week – but too long. It reached and settled into a bunker he hadn't considered within range.

The American then proceeded to hit a superb 5-iron to a distance – 6 feet – he'd been holing out from all week. Norman played out of what may come to be known as 'Norman's Bunker' into another nearer the green, and from there blasted through the green out of bounds. Calcavecchia had three putts for the championship to beat Grady, almost a spectator in these final stages.

It had been a different story for him and others in earlier rounds.

A nonentity on the European Tour, Wayne Stephens, led the first day with a 66. As so often happens, he then gradually toppled down the field – his finishing position 17 behind the winner, being the same as reigning champion Ballesteros.

Grady moved to the top on the second day with a 67 to follow his opening 68. One behind were Payne Stewart (72, 65 – a new course record) and Tom Watson (69, 68), still seeking to tie Harry Vardon's record six wins.

In a Ryder Cup year the Europeans were not showing, with only Mark James of the top 14 a likely team member. In James's second round 70 there was a moment to savour when he topped his drive and then hit a duck slice for his second shot. Even so, he still managed a 5.

Grady was not thought a likely winner. Although he had won the Westchester Classic in the USA in recent weeks, he was more renowned for having amassed 27 second place finishes in his career – and few wins. No one was noticing the eventual champion (71, 68) at all.

Instead the chances of Watson looked promising, the certainty of his play in the early 1980s returning. After the third day his hopes were high. With a 68 he lay on 205, one behind Grady. Stewart was on 206 and Feherty, Fred Couples and Calcavecchia on 207.

On the final day Norman, starting seven behind the leader, determined to "go for everything". Often that doesn't last. A bogey early on and any player in that frame of mind quickly changes to thinking of international plane schedules.

But Norman had a blazing start – birdies on the first six holes. Thereafter, he kept his score going, after dropping a shot on the little 8th, with birdies on the 11th, 12th and 16th. His eventual 64 ranks as a great last round alongside Palmer's 65 in the 1960 US Open, or Miller's 63 in the same championship in 1973. The crucial difference being, of course, that they went on to win.

Calcavecchia, well aware that he was in with a chance, was not really noticed when he freaked a huge putt in to save his par on the 11th, but there was a stir at his play on the 12th. He sent his second shot into a poor lie on a bank above the green and then lobbed his next clean into the hole for a birdie.

He still had ground to make up and did so by reaching the long 16th with a driver second and hitting a brilliant 8-iron close to the flag on the last. The resulting tie led to that play-off.

Grady, just behind, did little wrong but faltered in the second nine, while Watson's chances faded with slight frailties in the middle of his round.

This was a championship where a forward move had to be made. Watson (72) and Grady (71) only held their ground.

Ballesteros

Wayne Grady

Mark Calcavecchia

Norman from a bunker

Grady

Tom Watson

Nick Faldo

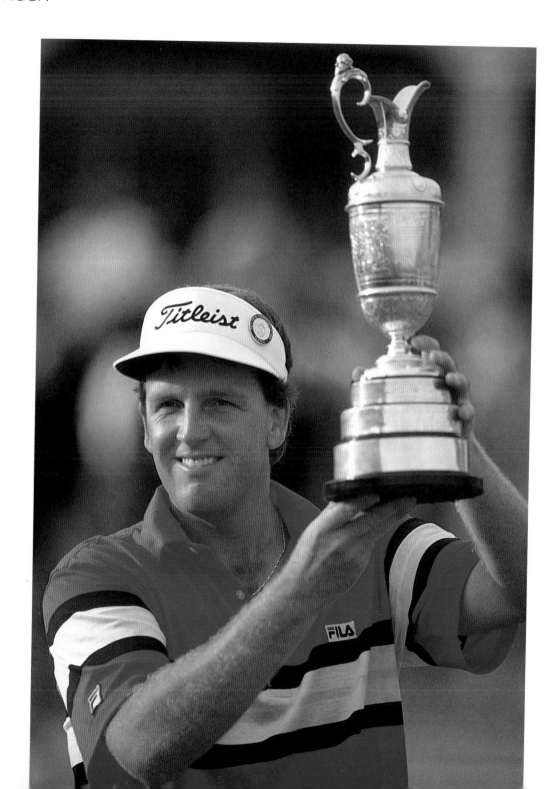

THE OPEN

It's not even a half truth, but history will record that this Open was won and lost in the third round when Nick Faldo put Greg Norman to the sword. I say this simply because, though Faldo did indeed lead the field by five strokes at the end of the third day, there were eighteen holes still to play.

But let's look at this third round in more detail. When the two went out last, Faldo had put in scores of 67, 65, Norman a pair of 66s. Their totals of 132 equalled the best ever start in the Open, made by Henry Cotton back in 1934. On current form and performance they were the world's best two golfers and here they were, four strokes clear of their closest pursuers: Craig Parry of Australia and Payne Stewart. This was particularly remarkable because St Andrews was playing easily, at the mercy of lesser performers. In two rounds of golf you could count the number of players who failed to break 80 on the fingers of one hand and the 36-hole cut, one under par, was comfortably the lowest ever.

Usually the cream comes to the top when you have to drive straight to avoid punishing rough, or when strong winds demand excellence of ball control. On these two days a steady club golfer ought to have scored below his handicap.

After eight holes both Faldo and Norman had a couple of birdies, nothing special as the second nine is more testing. Norman, however, had a bogey on his card, the result of a three-putt. Then his troubles began to mount with three-putts on the 9th, 10th and 12th. Meanwhile, Faldo had birdied both 9th and 11th and was suddenly four strokes clear. He even gained more ground on the 12th. Driving into gorse, he took three shots to reach the green, but then single-putted for his par 4 while Norman took 5.

For the Australian the championship was almost over and it finished as he dropped shots on the 13th, 15th and 16th. He was back in 40 for a 76 and deserves much credit for coming back the next day in 69, two below Faldo's score — which didn't matter one jot.

Faldo came home with a 67 for a new record aggregate of 199. Others had lower rounds that third day — notably Paul Broadhurst, whose 63 equalled the lowest round ever in a major championship. More significant was Australian Ian Baker-Finch's 64, which brought him up to a tie for second place with Payne Stewart, who had his third 68.

At this point Faldo had three majors to his credit, coming from two play-offs for the Masters and the 1987 Muirfield Open which, to some extent, Paul Azinger had thrown away. His current position brought a new pressure — how absurd to throw away a five stroke lead!

He reassured himself on the very first hole by pitching almost dead for a birdie. Stewart did come up close for a few minutes and after a birdie at the 12th was only two strokes behind, but he then faded a little. When Faldo birdied the 15th he knew the rest would be a triumphal progress.

It was. He finished five ahead of Stewart and Mark McNulty, who had a closing 65. The only opponent Faldo failed to beat was the 17th hole, where he had his third bogey 5.

Norman (above)
Ian Baker-Finch (left),
Payne Stewart (right),

Mark McNulty

Faldo with his caddie Fanny Sunesson